Implementation of Anti-money Laundering Information Systems

Yong Li

authorHOUSE®

AuthorHouse™
1663 Liberty Drive
Bloomington, IN 47403
www.authorhouse.com
Phone: 1 (800) 839-8640

Published by AuthorHouse   05/12/2016

ISBN: 978-1-5246-0672-5 (sc)
ISBN: 978-1-5246-0671-8 (e)

Library of Congress Control Number: 2016907224

Print information available on the last page.

Legal Notes

Regulatory compliance is an ever changing space. In this book, only information of certain compliance topics is provided – not legal advice. For the latest anti-money laundering related laws and regulations, readers are advised to contact corresponding regulators or seek professional help if they are concerned about a specific issue in a particular jurisdiction.

Every precaution has been made in the preparation of this book to ensure the accuracy of the information presented, however, the publisher and the author assume no responsibility for errors or omissions, or for damages resulting from the use of the information contained herein. The advice and strategies contained herein may not be suitable for everyone's situation. Readers should consult with a professional where appropriate.

Designations used by organizations to distinguish their products are often claimed as trademarks. All trademarks in this book are trademarks of their respective owners. Rather than put a trademark symbol after every occurrence of a trademarked name, this book uses names in an editorial fashion only, and to the benefit of the trademark owner, with no intention of infringement of the trademark. Where such designations appear in this book, they have been printed with initial capital or all capital letters. Readers, however, should contact the appropriate organizations for more complete information regarding trademarks and registration.

Contents

Introduction

"If there is a book that you want to read, but it hasn't been written yet, you must be the one to write it."

— Toni Morrison

ABOUT THIS BOOK

As we all know there is no magical formula for implementing pain-free anti-money laundering (AML) information systems in financial services organizations. And we also know that sharing of knowledge and best practice is critical for compliance professionals in financial institutions (FIs) to combat money laundering and terrorist financing. There have been many books on AML compliance, most of them focus on statutory, legal, regulatory compliance and business subjects but very few (only some consulting firms' white papers, not books) touch the AML information systems (IS) technical implementation in great detail. This has motivated me to write an introductory book about AML information systems implementation, from a practitioner's point of view, to share the germane experience I have gained from my previous AML and other compliance projects/programs, as well as to share the accumulated knowledge I have learned from industry subject matter experts on both compliance side and Information Technology (IT) side. Hopefully this book could provide some practical details to address some pain points in AML information systems implementation for fellow AML compliance practitioners.

In this book, an AML information systems implementation refers to an implementation of brand new or enhanced/updated or migrated AML information systems.

The Target Audience and Scope of This Book

This book is intended for compliance professionals, IT professionals and business stakeholders who are working on AML or Financial Crime Risk Management information systems implementation. And hopefully anyone who is interested in AML or financial crime risk management information systems implementation could also use this book as one of the reference sources.

Most topics discussed in this book are for banks in the United States and Canada, but the principles and frameworks mentioned in the book could also be utilized in AML information systems implementations for insurance companies, asset/investment management firms and securities dealers/ brokers in North America or other jurisdictions even though different type financial institutions have different AML regulatory requirements in different jurisdictions.

In Chapter 2 and Chapter 3, an overview of the most common and important topics in AML compliance and related information systems is provided, but readers are assumed to have some basic knowledge of financial services industry and information technology.

This book focuses on the AML information systems technical implementation, especially the implementation/project planning, and current state, future state, gap analysis as well some technical solutions/ practical approaches. The following three compliance software modules are out of the scope of this book:

1. The implementation or integration of an organization's Governance, Risk and Compliance (GRC) module.

Today, many financial institutions adapt the holistic GRC approach to comply with the numerous statutory, legal, and regulatory requirements. But GRC functions are not necessarily administered by the AML compliance program but rather by the enterprise risk management (ERM) department in an organization. Also, the implementation of a GRC platform is not dependent upon and is not necessary to have been completed earlier than the implementation of AML information systems in financial institutions.

2. The implementation or integration of an organization's AML training module.

Per the regulatory requirements, most financial institutions already have AML training programs in place prior to the AML information systems implementation, and very likely, other department(s) in the organization might own the training software and be responsible for the administration and coordination of training software usage.

3. The implementation or integration of an organization's internal auditing module.

Internal auditing tools are usually not dedicated to AML compliance only. And the implementation of internal auditing tools is very likely not dependent upon the implementation of AML information systems in financial institutions.

The technical discussions in this book are software vendor agnostic and platform neutral. Although the emphasis of this book is on AML information systems implementation, I strongly believe the planning methodologies and solution approaches could also be applied to the implementation of financial crime risk management information systems/ modules in the following areas:

- Anti-Bribery and Anti-Corruption (ABAC) (Foreign Corrupt Practices Act (FCPA) in U.S. and Corruption of Foreign Public Officials Act (CFPOA)/Canadian Criminal Code in Canada)

- Foreign Account Tax Compliance Act (FATCA)

- Fraud (including but not limited to banking fraud, investment fraud, employee fraud, tax fraud, senior/elder abuse, identity theft and other financial frauds)

- Market Conduct

- Cyber security related financial crimes

Of course, each type of financial crime has its own characteristics and red flags, but all of them do share many commonalities, in particular some common information/data elements about customers, accounts, transactions and etc.

How This Book Is Organized

The rest of this book is organized as follows. Chapter 2 provides an overview of AML laws and regulations in the United States and Canada first, and then emphasizes the key components of a sound AML compliance program in a financial institution. Chapter 3 covers an overview of key AML information systems available in the market, and then looks at some common features in two key system components, watch-list screening and transaction monitoring modules. Chapter 4 describes some challenges of AML information systems implementation first, and then proposes a unified implementation planning framework: from stakeholder analysis and the implementation governance model, up to activity breakdown for implementation planning and some other implementation management considerations. Chapter 5 discusses the practical solution approaches in the whole life cycle of AML information systems implementation – pre-deployment, deployment and post-deployment stages. In the pre-deployment part, topics of the current state, future state and gap analysis, business requirements, Commercial Off-The-Shelf (COTS) systems/vendors selection, systems specifications, architecture and design, systems building and testing are discussed. In the deployment part, topics of data loading/migration, configuration settings, production readiness check, information security, business continuity planning (BCP) and disaster recovery planning (DRP), documentation and training are discussed. In the post-deployment part, topics of support and operations, performance reporting and benchmarking, calibration and enhancements are discussed. The appendixes start with Appendix A, which covers an introduction of entity resolution and its applications to AML compliance. Appendix B provides the background information about the major funds transfer systems in the United States and Canada that are critical for AML compliance.

ACKNOWLEDGEMENTS

I would like to thank those people who were influential either directly or indirectly in the existence of this book, especial my former/current colleagues and supervisors Christine West, Brenda Meyer, Alyssa Burton, Carol Ann Levesque, Colin Simpson, Mike Jensen, Eugenio (Gene) DiMira, Rob Jones, Christine Reid, Bob Bray, Betty Havasi, Dave Sepa, Michael Rand, Raquel Garcia, Aanchal Gulia, Fiona Cowden, Lynne Butterworth, Gokul Kallambunathil, Mark Scarmozzino, Rachel Workman, Peter Romano, Uday Gulvadi, Vishnu Vellampalli, Siyu Tu, Dianjie Hou, Maolin He, Andrew Davies, Frits Fraase Storm, Pierre Isensee, Henk Huisman, Ryan Fifield, Ken Wolckenhauer, Richard Hoogenboom, Gloria Chu and many others. I also appreciate Paul McKay, Richard Hogeveen, John McEachen, Tim Traill, Brad Caron, Jeff Lapierre, Gord Willms, Andy White, Linda Buchanan, Dianne Lapierre, Jim McInnis, Kathleen Pettit, Sharon Murrell-Foster, Maureen Hurley, Gillian Embro, Wendy Voisin, Salvatore Cangialosi, Mahesh Viswanathan and other senior managers for their directly or indirectly guidance and support in my previous projects and programs.

I am greatly indebted to Michael Gerrie and Anthony Shum for their readings of the manuscript and extremely valuable suggestions. And of course, any remaining mistakes and errors are purely mine.

And, I would also like to thank the AuthorHouse team, Mae Genson, Rowella Alvaro and Joseph Elas for their help and patience in the editing of this book.

Last but not least, I would like to thank my wife, Annie, my daughter, Rita, and my extended family members around the world for their understanding and support throughout my career.

Anti-money Laundering Compliance

"Money laundering is a very sophisticated crime and we must be equally sophisticated."

— Janet Reno

WHAT IS MONEY LAUNDERING AND TERRORIST FINANCING?

The United Nations (UN) defines Money Laundering (ML) as "any act or attempted act to disguise the source of money or assets derived from criminal activity." Essentially, money laundering is the process of making dirty money look clean.

Terrorist Financing (TF) provides funds for terrorist activities. The main objective of terrorist activities is to intimidate a population or compel a government to do, or refrain from doing, something.

Money laundering and terrorist financing share one common element – they are both keen to disguise the source and/or destination of funds.

Terrorist groups seek to develop and utilize sources of funds to obtain materials and other logistical items needed to commit terrorist acts.

The process that disguises a legitimate source of funds that are to be used for illegal purposes (in the future) is called "reverse money laundering"[1]. Since cash is anonymous and its source is nearly undetectable, from time to time, terrorist groups or criminals perform the reverse money laundering transactions to accumulate cash for illegal purposes.

The United Nations Office on Drugs and Crime (UNODC) conducted a study to determine the magnitude of illicit funds generated by drug trafficking and organized crimes, and to investigate to what extent these funds are laundered. The report[2] estimated that in 2009, criminal proceeds amounted to 3.6% of global gross domestic product (GDP), with 2.7% (or 1.6 trillion U.S. dollars) being laundered. This falls within the widely quoted estimate by the International Monetary Fund (IMF), which stated in 1998 that the aggregate size of money laundering in the world could be somewhere between 2% and 5% of the world's GDP.

Money laundering and terrorist financing can have potentially devastating economic, security and social consequences.

The Stages of Money Laundering

There are three recognized stages that can occur simultaneously in the money laundering process: Placement, Layering and Integration.

Placement – the physical disposal of cash derived from criminal activity and the initial entry of the "dirty" cash or proceeds of crime into the financial system.

---

[1]   Stefan D. Cassella, "Reverse Money Laundering", Journal of Money Laundering Control, Vol.7 No.1, pp.92 - 94, 2003

[2]   The United Nations Office on Drugs and Crime (UNODC) Research Report, "Estimating illicit financial flows resulting from drug trafficking and other transnational organized crimes", October 2011

Layering – (sometimes referred to as structuring) the separation of illicit proceeds from their source by layers of financial transactions intended to obscure the audit trail and sever the link with the original crime.

Integration – the money is returned to the criminal from what seem to be legitimate sources of funds. Having been placed initially as cash and layered through a number of financial transactions, the criminal proceeds are now fully integrated into the financial system and can be used for any purpose.

The following is a real life example of money laundering[3]:

On September 29, 2014, in Miami, Florida, USA, Alvaro López Tardón, of Miami Beach and Madrid, Spain, was sentenced to 150 years in prison and ordered to pay a $14 million forfeiture money judgment and $2 million fine. Tardón was also ordered to forfeit a significant number of assets, including luxury real estate, cars and bank accounts. Tardón was convicted on one count of conspiracy to commit money laundering and 13 substantive counts of money laundering. According to court documents, Tardón was the head of an international narcotics trafficking and money laundering syndicate which distributed over 7,500 kilograms of South American cocaine in Madrid and laundered over $14 million in narcotics proceeds in Miami by buying high-end real estate, luxury and exotic automobiles and other high-end items. The proceeds were smuggled into Miami by couriers, wire transferred to South Florida by co-conspirators, wire transferred to third parties internationally on behalf of Tardón, and wire transferred directly to Tardón and his co-conspirators in Miami through Tardón's exotic car dealership and other companies controlled by him located in Madrid, Spain.

In this example, all three money laundering stages were involved:

- Placement – the money launderer(s) smuggled and deposited "dirty money" directly into bank accounts or purchased high value goods.

---

[3] "Examples of Money Laundering Investigations - Fiscal Year 2014" are available at https://www.irs.gov/uac/Examples-of-Money-Laundering-Investigations-Fiscal-Year-2014 (retrieved on May 1, 2016)

- Layering – deposited cash was wire transferred from one bank account to another internationally.

- Integration – laundered proceeds were put back into the economy to create the perception of legitimacy by investing the funds in real estate, luxury assets or other business ventures as well as by reselling high value goods for payment by check or bank transfer.

As the reference [6] pointed out, not all money laundering transactions involve all three distinct stages, and some may indeed involve more. Nevertheless, the three-stage classification is a useful decomposition of what can sometimes be a complex process.

Overview of AML Laws and Regulations in the United States and Canada

U.S. Laws and Regulations

The legal regime for money laundering controls that is applicable to U.S. financial institutions consists mainly of the U.S. Bank Secrecy Act (BSA) and BSA regulations, the USA Patriot Act, the U.S. Treasury Department Office of Foreign Asset Control (OFAC) regulations and the U.S. money laundering laws (including the Money Laundering Control Act). These statutes and regulations direct banks and other financial institutions to establish and maintain procedures reasonably designed to detect and report money laundering, large cash, and other suspicious transactions to the U.S. government.

There are several U.S. federal agencies that are responsible for the oversight of the various financial institutions operating in the U.S. These include the Board of Governors of the Federal Reserve System commonly known as the Federal Reserve Board (FRB), Federal Deposit Insurance Corporation (FDIC), National Credit Union Administration (NCUA), Office of the Comptroller of the Currency (OCC), the Consumer Financial Protection Bureau (CFPB), and State Liaison Committee (SLC). And the SLC includes representatives from the Conference of State Bank Supervisors

(CSBS), the American Council of State Savings Supervisors (ACSSS), and the National Association of State Credit Union Supervisors (NASCUS).

The Federal Financial Institutions Examination Council (FFIEC), consisting of these U.S. regulators issues BSA/AML Examination Manuals[4] that offer guidance to examiners for carrying out BSA/AML and Office of Foreign Assets Control (OFAC) examinations. The BSA/AML Examination Manual includes guidance on identifying and controlling risks associated with money laundering and terrorist financing.

Many U.S. banks and other financial institutions use the FFIEC BSA/AML Examination Manual as a guidance document for implementing and designing a risk-based AML program and monitoring efforts.

The FFIEC BSA/AML Examination Manual contains an overview of BSA/AML compliance program requirements, BSA/AML risks and risk management expectations, industry sound practices, and examination procedures.

Banks and other financial institutions are subject to BSA reporting and record keeping requirements set forth in regulations issued by the U.S. Treasury Department. They include but not limited to requirements applicable to cash and monetary instrument (MI) transactions and funds transfers, Currency Transaction Report (CTR) filing and exemption rules, and due diligence, certification, and other requirements for foreign correspondent and private banking accounts.

Financial institutions are required by federal regulations to file a Suspicious Activity Report (SAR) no later than 30 calendar days after the date of the initial detection by the reporting financial institution of facts that may constitute a basis for filing a report.

---

[4] "Bank Secrecy Act/ Anti-Money Laundering Examination Manual (2014 Edition) V2" is available at
https://www.ffiec.gov/bsa_aml_infobase/documents/BSA_AML_Man_2014_v2.pdf
(retrieved on May 1, 2016)

The BSA requires the filing of a report of international transportation of Currency and Monetary Instruments (CMIR) by any person (including a bank), who physically transports, mails, ships, or causes to be physically transported, mailed, or shipped, currency or other monetary instrument in an aggregate amount exceeding $10,000 on any one occasion, whether that transportation is into or out of the United States.

According to the Egmont Group, an informal international network of financial intelligence units, a financial intelligence unit (FIU) is defined as a national center for the receipt and analysis of: (a) suspicious transaction reports; and (b) other information relevant to money laundering, associated predicate offences and financing of terrorism, and for the dissemination of the results of that analysis.

The Financial Crimes Enforcement Network (FinCEN) is a bureau of the U. S. Department of the Treasury and, as the U.S. Financial Intelligence Unit (FIU), collects and analyzes information about financial transactions in order to combat domestic and international money laundering, terrorist financing, and other financial crimes.

CANADIAN LAWS AND REGULATIONS

The legal regime for money laundering controls that is applicable to Canadian financial institutions is the Proceeds of Crime (Money Laundering) and Terrorist Financing Act (PCMLTFA). There are five regulations under the PCMLTFA:

1. The Proceeds of Crime (Money Laundering) and Terrorist Financing Suspicious Transaction Reporting Regulations

2. The Proceeds of Crime (Money Laundering) and Terrorist Financing Regulations

3. The Cross-Border Currency and Monetary Instruments Reporting Regulations

4. The Proceeds of Crime (Money Laundering) and Terrorist Financing Registration Regulations

5. The Proceeds of Crime (Money Laundering) and Terrorist Financing Administrative Monetary Penalties Regulations

Canada continues to work through the Financial Action Task Force (FATF) — an inter-governmental body Canada helped create in 1989 that sets standards and promotes effective implementation of legal, regulatory and operational measures for combating money laundering and terrorist financing, to develop common international standards that stay ahead of criminals on a global scale while making Canadian regime even stronger.

In Canada, the Office of the Superintendent of Financial Institutions (OSFI) was created in 1987 to regulate and supervise financial institutions and private pension plans subject to federal oversight (up to the time this book was written, the Canadian securities industry is not regulated by OSFI but by provincial regulators and self-regulatory organizations).

The Financial Transactions and Reports Analysis Centre of Canada (FINTRAC) is Canada's financial intelligence unit (FIU), which covers not only banks, but also securities dealers and beyond.

In addition to OSFI guidance (including guidelines and advisories such as "B-8 Deterring and Detecting Money Laundering and Terrorist Financing"), banks, foreign bank branches and other financial institutions in Canada use FINTRAC guidelines as guidance documents for implementing and designing a risk-based AML program and monitoring efforts.

As of the end of 2015, the complete list of all FINTRAC guidelines is as follows[5]:

- Guideline 1: Backgrounder

- Guideline 2: Suspicious Transactions

---

[5] All FINTRAC Guidelines are available at http://www.fintrac.gc.ca/publications/guide/guide-eng.asp (retrieved on May 1, 2016)

- Guideline 3A: Submitting Suspicious Transaction Reports to FINTRAC Electronically

- Guideline 3B: Submitting Suspicious Transaction Reports to FINTRAC by Paper

- Guideline 4: Implementation of a Compliance Regime

- Guideline 5: Submitting Terrorist Property Reports

- Guideline 6: Record Keeping and Client Identification

  - 6A: Life Insurance Companies, Brokers and Agents

  - 6B: Real Estate

  - 6C: Money Services Businesses

  - 6D: Accountants

  - 6E: Securities Dealers

  - 6F: Casinos

  - 6G: Financial Entities

  - 6H: Agents of the Crown that Sell or Redeem Money Orders

  - 6I: Dealers in Precious Metals and Stones

  - 6J: British Columbia Notaries

- Guideline 7A: Submitting Large Cash Transaction Reports to FINTRAC Electronically

- Guideline 7B: Submitting Large Cash Transaction Reports to FINTRAC by Paper

- Guideline 8A: Submitting Non-SWIFT Electronic Funds Transfer Reports to FINTRAC Electronically

- Guideline 8B: Submitting SWIFT Electronic Funds Transfer Reports to FINTRAC

- Guideline 8C: Submitting Non-SWIFT Electronic Funds Transfer Reports to FINTRAC by Paper

- Guideline 9: Alternative to Large Cash Transaction Reports to FINTRAC

- Guideline 10A: Submitting Casino Disbursement Reports to FINTRAC Electronically

- Guideline 10B Submitting Casino Disbursement Reports to FINTRAC by Paper

Despite the fact there are many commonalities and similarities between U.S. AML regulations and Canadian AML regulations, there are some differences between two AML regimes, not only with regard to some terminologies (i.e., you say 'To-may-to' and I say 'To-mah-to' things, such as CTR vs. LCTR (Large Cash Transaction Report), SAR vs. STR (Suspicious Transaction Report)), but also in subtleness of detailed requirements. Readers are advised to contact corresponding regulators or seek professional help if they are concerned about a specific AML related issue in a particular jurisdiction.

THE COST OF NON-COMPLIANCE

The costs and consequences of non-compliance within financial institutions are greater than ever before. Monetary fines, while huge and still growing, can be the least of the costs imposed on financial institutions. Any violation of AML regulations could lead to criminal charges and reputational risk for a financial institution.

In 2012, HSBC agreed to pay $1.9 billion and entered into a five-year deferred-prosecution agreement to settle allegations including that it failed to catch at least $881 million in drug-trafficking proceeds laundered through its U.S. bank and that its staff stripped data from transactions with Iran, Libya and Sudan to evade U.S. sanctions[6].

In July 2015, Citigroup said it would liquidate and shut its Banamex USA operations and pay $140 million to regulators who alleged the bank did not correct weaknesses they had found in 2012 in its AML programs. As of November 20, 2015 Citigroup is still under orders from its two main regulators, the Federal Reserve and the Office of the Comptroller of the Currency (OCC), to fix its AML practices and is the subject of a U.S. Justice Department investigation that focuses on money-laundering controls at Banamex USA[7].

Increased regulatory scrutiny and complexities of regulatory changes as well as customer distrust are set to continue as a result of the widespread compliance failures.

KEY COMPONENTS OF AN AML COMPLIANCE PROGRAM

In the U.S., the FFIEC BSA/AML Examination Manual specifies that the BSA/AML compliance program for a bank must have the following minimum four pillars (and the FinCEN's latest CDD final rule creates a fifth "pillar" – Risk-Based Due Diligence):

- A system of internal controls to ensure ongoing compliance.

- Independent testing of BSA/AML compliance.

- Designate an individual or individuals responsible for managing BSA/AML compliance (BSA/AML compliance officer).

- Training for appropriate personnel.

---

[6]   Rachel Louise Ensign, "The Chemist Who Took On HSBC", The Wall Street Journal, February 29, 2016

[7]   Alan Katz and Dakin Campbell, "Inside the Money Laundering Scheme That Citi Overlooked for Years", Bloomberg Markets, November 20, 2015

In addition, a Customer Identification Program (CIP) must be included as part of the BSA/AML compliance program for a bank operating in the U.S.

In Canada, FINTRAC "Guideline 4: Implementation of a Compliance Regime" (the latest version came into effect on June 19, 2015) specifies five requirements of the AML compliance program (the AML compliance regime) for a bank and beyond:

- The appointment of a compliance officer;

- The development and application of compliance policies and procedures;

- An assessment and documentation of risks related to money laundering and terrorist financing, as well as the documentation and implementation of mitigation measures to deal with those risks;

- An ongoing compliance training program; and

- A review of the compliance policies and procedures to test their effectiveness (the review has to be done every two years).

In both U.S. and Canada, an effective AML compliance program has many key elements, including but not limited to a sound risk management program, and a transaction monitoring system to detect large currency transactions and suspicious activities.

THREE LINES OF DEFENSE IN *AML* COMPLIANCE

The Basel Committee on Banking Supervision (BCBS), an international body established by the central bank governors of the Group of Ten countries in 1974, is the primary global standard-setter for the prudential regulation of banks and provides an international forum for regular cooperation on banking supervisory matters. In January 2014, BCBS published "*Sound management of risks related to money laundering and financing of terrorism*"

(BCBS 275) and it specifies the three lines of defense (3LoD) in the context of AML/CFT (Combating the Financing of Terrorism):

- The business units (e.g. front office, customer-facing activity) are the first line of defense in charge of identifying, assessing and controlling the risks of their business

- The Chief Officer in charge of AML/CFT, as part of the second line of defense, should have the responsibility for ongoing monitoring of the fulfilment of all AML/CFT duties by the bank, and the business interests of a bank should in no way be opposed to the effective discharge of the above-mentioned responsibilities of the Chief AML/CFT Officer

- Internal audit, the third line of defense, plays an important role in independently evaluating the risk management and controls, and discharges its responsibility to the audit committee of the board of directors (BOD) or a similar oversight body through periodic evaluations of the effectiveness of compliance with AML/CFT policies and procedures. In many countries, external auditors also have an important role to play in evaluating banks' internal controls and procedures in the course of their financial audits, and in confirming that they are compliant with AML/CFT regulations and supervisory practice

As it was pointed out by the reference [12], each line of defense actually shows the comparative position to the proximity to business, regularity of review and degree of independence:

	Decreasing independence↑	Increasing proximity to business↑	Increasing regularity of review↑
The first line of defense			
The second line of defense			
The third line of defense			

Table-2-1 The Three Lines of Defense in AML Compliance

CUSTOMER ACCEPTANCE AND MAINTENANCE RULES

In U.S., the FFIEC BSA/AML Examination Manual calls comprehensive customer due diligence (CDD) the "cornerstone of a strong BSA/AML compliance program" and notes that CDD policies, procedures, and processes should cover all customers, with an emphasis on those that present a higher risk for money laundering and terrorist financing (ML/TF). The Know Your Customer (KYC) provision is a financial regulatory rule that is mandated by the Bank Secrecy Act and the USA PATRIOT Act of 2003 and covers the Customer Identification Program (CIP) requirements, CDD for all customers, and enhanced due diligence (EDD) for higher risk customers. The objective of the KYC rule is to reduce the possibility of the financial system being used for money laundering and terrorist financing activities.

The Customer Identification Program (CIP) is a mandatory requirement[8] that is stipulated by Section 326 of the USA PATRIOT Act (to collect name, physical address, and government identification number for all customers along with date of birth for individuals and verification of the customer's identity). The objective of each firm's CIP program is to enable the firm to form a reasonable belief that it knows the true identity of each customer. Each firm's CIP needs to be risk-based and in accordance with the firm's size, type of business, customer type, and overall risk. CIP must be in writing (well-documented) and be part of a company's overall AML program.

CDD (customer due diligence) on the other hand is the second phase of the overall KYC process. It begins after CIP, and it involves conducting detailed analysis and assessment of a new customer from an AML risk perspective (i.e., low, medium or high risk), that is, tries to understand the nature of the customer's activities and assess ML/TF risk associated with the customer.

---

[8]   In U.S., as of May 1, 2016, CIP requirements are not mandatory for insurance companies..

Enhanced due diligence (EDD) is also called special due diligence, which refers to collecting additional information for higher risk customers to gain a deeper understanding of customer activities to mitigate the heightened ML/TF risks.

In Canada, FINTRAC guidelines (especially the following two guidelines) explain the detailed Know Your Customer (KYC) requirements:

- Guideline 6G: Record Keeping and Client Identification for Financial Entities

- Guideline 4: Implementation of a Compliance Regime

Please note that FINTRAC guidelines require ongoing monitoring for two types of business relationships between a financial institution and a client - within an account (account-based business relationship) or outside of an account (non-account-based business relationship).

Both in U.S. and Canada, covered financial institutions[9] are required to identify and keep an entity's beneficial ownership information.

THE RISK BASED APPROACH AND RISK ASSESSMENTS

According to the inter-governmental body Financial Action Task Force (FATF), a Risk Based Approach (RBA) to Anti-Money Laundering/ Countering the Financing of Terrorism (AML/CFT) means that countries, competent authorities and financial institutions, are expected to identify, assess and understand the ML/TF risks to which they are exposed and take AML/CFT measures commensurate to those risks in order to mitigate them effectively.

In U.S., Risk Based Approach AML/CFT measures specified in the FFIEC BSA/AML Examination Manual for a bank or a financial institution

---

[9]   Currently in U.S., private bank accounts and correspondent accounts for certain foreign financial institutions are required. On May 6, 2016, the FinCEN released its final rule on beneficial ownership with respect to CDD requirements..

include, but not limited to, the following (please refer to FFIEC BSA/AML Examination Manual for more details):

- Freezing assets under U.S. jurisdiction against targeted individuals and entities such as foreign countries, regimes, terrorists, international narcotics traffickers, and those engaged in certain activities such as the proliferation of weapons of mass destruction (WMD or WoMD) or transnational organized crime

- Sharing information with regulatory authorities, law enforcement and other financial institutions

- Collection, verification and ongoing tracking of customers' and beneficial owners' information, especially the high risk customers discussed in the FFIEC BSA/AML Examination Manual (such as Politically Exposed Persons (PEPs), Nonresident alien (NRA), Nongovernmental organizations (NGOs) and charities (foreign and domestic), etc.)

- Identification and ongoing monitoring of high risk product types and transaction types, such as

  ○ Cash (e.g., large cash transactions over $10,000, cross-border movement of cash)

  ○ Funds transfers (e.g., cross-border wire or Automated Clearing House (ACH) transfers)

  ○ Prepaid access (e.g., prepaid and payroll cards)

  ○ Monetary instruments (MIs, e.g., official bank checks, cashier's checks, money orders, and traveler's checks)

- Identification and ongoing monitoring of high risk geographic locations (either international or domestic) unique to the bank or the financial institution and their customers

In Canada, FINTRAC published "Guidance on the Risk-Based Approach to Combatting Money laundering and Terrorist Financing" that outlines the six steps of RBA cycle for an AML/Anti-Terrorist Financing (ATF) reporting entity:

1. Identification of the inherent risks (business-based risk assessment along with the relationship-based risk assessment) - the intrinsic risks of events or circumstances that exist before the application of controls or mitigation measures;

2. Setting the risk tolerance;

3. Creating risk-reduction measures and key controls;

4. Evaluating the residual risks - the levels of risks that remain after the implementation of mitigation measures and controls;

5. Implementing the risk-based approach; and

6. Reviewing the risk-based approach.

Similar to the U.S. FFIEC BSA/AML Examination Manual, FINTRAC's "Guidance on the Risk-Based Approach to Combatting Money laundering and Terrorist Financing" provides the guidelines to the risk assessment of business activities and clients using certain prescribed elements:

*   Products, services and delivery channels;

*   Geography;

*   Clients and business relationships; and

*   Other relevant factors.

A financial institution could have multiple risk assessments, such as OFAC/Sanction risk assessment, Line of Business (LOB) risk assessment for a LOB or a business division, and aggregated enterprise wide risk assessment.

Typically, a risk assessment may contain the following information for each identified risk:

- Risk type/category

- Inherent risk

- Mitigation measures and controls

- Risk mitigation factors

- Residual risk

- Risk direction/trending

In U.S., the FFIEC BSA/AML Examination Manual (especially the following subsection and appendices) provides detailed information about risk assessments:

- "Identification of Specific Risk Categories" subsection

- Appendix I: Risk Assessment Link to the BSA/AML Compliance Program

- Appendix J: Quantity of Risk Matrix

- Appendix K: Customer Risk Versus Due Diligence and Suspicious Activity Monitoring

In Canada, FINTRAC (especially the following guidelines) provides detailed information about risk assessments:

- Guidance on the Risk-Based Approach to Combatting Money laundering and Terrorist Financing

- Guideline 4: Implementation of a Compliance Regime

- FINTRAC Policy Interpretations : Ongoing Monitoring (FAQ)

ISO 19600:2014 AND OTHER COMPLIANCE FRAMEWORKS

There is an international standard ISO 19600:2014 for compliance management systems. ISO 19600:2014 provides guidance for establishing, developing, implementing, evaluating, maintaining and improving an effective and responsive compliance management system (or compliance program) within an organization.

ISO 19600:2014 is risk-based and built on the principles of good governance, proportionality, transparency and sustainability.

The key themes of ISO 19600:2014 are as follows:

1. Context of the organization – compliance programs need to understand the environment in which the organizations operate, compliance obligations which are mandatory (e.g., legislations) and voluntary (e.g., internal codes of conduct), internal and external stakeholders' compliance expectations, as well as organizational risk appetites;

2. Leadership – the Board, Senior Management and all managers are accountable for compliance, not just the managers who run the compliance programs. Compliance programs need to ensure the actions taken by the leaders promote a compliance culture;

3. Planning – compliance programs should be planned and developed within the context of organizations' market environment, objectives, strategic direction and organizational values;

4. Support – compliance programs need to have sufficient resources, effective training for all staff, and adequate documentation;

5. Operation – compliance programs need to have operation related policies, procedures and controls in place. And operational targets need to align with compliance obligations;

6. Performance evaluation – compliance programs need to have a process (including effective reviews and audits) for evaluating and assessing the programs; and

7. Improvement – compliance programs require continuous improvement based on regular reviews of changing market environment, changing legislations, changing risks and internal controls.

Although the ISO 19600:2014 guidelines are generic to compliance management (i.e., not limited to AML compliance programs only and not limited to financial institutions only), an AML compliance program could apply certain guidelines in ISO 19600:2014 based on the size, structure, nature and complexity of the organization.

In Canada, some financial institutions also follow the spirit of OSFI E-13 Guideline "Regulatory Compliance Management (RCM)"[10] in their AML programs based on a variety of factors: size; ownership structure; nature, scope and complexity of operations; corporate strategy; risk profile; and geographical locations.

The basic elements of a sound RCM framework are key controls, including oversight functions. At a minimum, OSFI expects the RCM framework to include the following items (administered through a methodology that establishes clear lines of responsibility and a mechanism for holding individuals accountable):

1. Role of the Chief Compliance Officer (CCO);

2. Procedures for identifying, risk assessing, communicating, effectively managing and mitigating regulatory compliance risk and maintaining knowledge of applicable regulatory requirements;

3. Day-to-day compliance procedures;

---

[10] OSFI E-13 Guideline "Regulatory Compliance Management (RCM)" is available at http://www.osfi-bsif.gc.ca/Eng/Docs/e13.pdf (retrieved on May 1, 2016)

4. Independent monitoring and testing procedures;

5. Internal reporting;

6. Role of Internal Audit or other independent review function;

7. Adequate documentation;

8. Role of Senior Management, and

9. Role of the Board.

Many other industry methodologies and frameworks are used in AML compliance programs. For example, the following IT and quality management frameworks could be considered to improve KYC processes[11]:

- CMM - Capability Maturity Model

- ITIL - the Information Technology Infrastructure Library for service management

- COSO (the Committee of Sponsoring Organizations of the Treadway Commission) and COBIT (Control Objectives for Information and Related Technology) - internal control–integrated and enterprise IT governance and management frameworks

- Lean - a customer-centric methodology used to continuously improve any process through the elimination of waste in everything performed in the process; it is based on the ideas of "Continuous Incremental Improvement" and "Respect for People"

- Agile Methodology - an iterative, incremental method of managing the design and build activities for engineering, information technology, and other business areas in a highly flexible and interactive manner

---

[11] For detailed discussions, please refer to Patrick Ryan, "The need for improvement", ACAMS Today, Vol. 11 No. 4, pp 38 – 40, September-November 2012

- Six Sigma - a disciplined, data-driven approach and methodology for eliminating defects (driving toward six standard deviations between the mean and the nearest specification limit) in any process

- Balanced Scorecard - a strategic planning and management system that is used extensively in business and industry, government, and nonprofit organizations worldwide to align business activities to the vision and strategy of the organization, improve internal and external communications, and monitor organization performance against strategic goals

Among numerous of methodologies and frameworks, the best one is the one that fits a financial institution's overall environment and compliance requirements.

Chapter 3

Key Components and Functions of AML Information Systems

"A great deal of creativity is about pattern recognition, and what you need to discern patterns is tons of data. Your mind collects that data by taking note of random details and anomalies easily seen every day: quirks and changes that, eventually, add up to insights."

— Margaret Heffernan

There are few basic types of software components addressing AML compliance requirements, for example:

- Watch-list and negative news/adverse media screening

- Transaction monitoring

- Case management and workflow

- CTR/LCTR and SAR/STR reporting

Although many AML software components work hand in hand, in this chapter, they are grouped and discussed according to two fundamental AML business requirements:

- Know Your Customer (KYC) compliance – including sanctions, watch-list and adverse media screening

- Ongoing monitoring – including but not limited to unusual transaction monitoring, case management & workflow and CTR/ LCTR & SAR/STR reporting

As it was mentioned in Chapter 1, the implementation and integration with enterprise GRC, AML training software and internal auditing tools would be out of the scope of this book.

In today's IT world, software could be deployed in three models: as an on-premises solution; as a SaaS (Software as a Service) service; as a hybrid SaaS, that is, software is deployed as a SaaS service and/or as an on-premises solution, and those instances would co-exist, securely communicate between each other, let each be a seamless extension of each other. Most leading commercial AML platforms in the market usually support all three deployment models.

WATCH-LIST AND MEDIA SCREENING

The core system for KYC compliance is the watch-list and adverse media screening software, which is used by a financial institution in

- Customer on-boarding/ongoing monitoring (auditable) processes

- SWIFT (Society for Worldwide Interbank Financial Telecommunication), international wire and ACH payment screening

- Resolution of critical BSA/AML and KYC compliance requirements (CIP, CDD, EDD, including to identify terrorists, high risk PEPs, fraudsters and criminals)

- Mitigation of risk exposures with enhanced due diligence (EDD) data, such as Reputationally Exposed Persons (REPs) in adverse media (i.e., unfavorable information that can be found in a variety of reference sources)[12]

• Cost reduction by minimizing manual reviews due to false positives

Three elements are the key for effectively using watch-list and adverse media screening software: entity resolution based rules and workflow engine(s) provided by a software vendor or an internal IT group within a financial institution; authoritative watch-lists and negative news/adverse media reference sources provided by government/international bodies and/ or commercial companies; the complete customer information data sets available within the financial institution.

Due to the non-trivial nature of the entity resolution based rules and workflow engine(s), usually a financial institution would use an industry proven third party commercial watch-list and adverse media screening software instead of building a home-grown one. Please refer to Appendix A. for some technical discussions about entity resolution and some related challenges.

The required customer information data sets within a financial institution will be discussed in Chapter 5. And the rest of this section will focus on authoritative reference sources for watch-lists and adverse media.

OFAC SANCTIONS

As part of its enforcement efforts, the Office of Foreign Assets Control (OFAC) of the U.S. Department of the Treasury publishes a list of Specially Designated Nationals (SDN). The SDN may be:

• Individuals and companies owned or controlled by, or acting for or on behalf of, targeted countries

---

[12] Carol Stabile, "A new approach to adverse media for enhanced due diligence", ACAMS Today, Vol. 13 No. 2, pp 72 – 74, March-May 2014

- Individuals, groups, and entities, such as terrorists and narcotics traffickers designated under programs that are not country-specific

In addition to the SDN list, OFAC also publishes the Consolidated Sanctions List by offering all of its non-SDN sanctions lists in a consolidated set of data files. And the Consolidated Sanctions list has few data format versions: comma delimited, @ sign delimited, "|" (pipe) character delimited, fixed-width delimited, and XML (Extensible Markup Language) files.

After October 10, 2014, OFAC offers an improved web-based Sanctions List Search Tool (https://sanctionssearch.ofac.treas.gov/) by employing fuzzy logic on the name search field to look for potential matches on its SDN List and Consolidated Sanctions List.

OTHER WATCH-LISTS

FinCEN 314(a) List

In U.S., FinCEN provides a unique service to law enforcement to help locate financial assets and recent transactions by subjects of criminal investigations. FinCEN's regulations under Section 314(a) of the USA PATRIOT Act of 2001 enable U.S. federal, state, local, and foreign (European Union - EU) law enforcement agencies, through FinCEN, to reach out to more than 43,000 points of contact at more than 22,000 financial institutions to locate accounts and transactions of persons that may be involved in terrorism or money laundering[13].

FinCEN receives requests from law enforcement and upon review, sends notifications to designated contacts within financial institutions across the country once every 2 weeks informing them new information has been made available via a secure Internet web site (https://www.fincen. gov/314a/#/). The requests contain subject and business names, addresses, and as much identifying data as possible to assist the financial industry in

---

[13]   Financial Crimes Enforcement Network (FinCEN), "FinCEN's 314(a) Fact Sheet", February 2, 2016

searching their records. The financial institutions must query their records for data matches, including accounts maintained by the named subject during the preceding 12 months and transactions conducted within the last 6 months. Financial institutions have 2 weeks from the posting date of the request to respond with any positive matches.

PEP List

In U.S., according to FFIEC BSA/AML Examination Manual, the term "politically exposed person" (PEP) generally includes a current or former senior foreign political figure, their immediate family, and their close associates. More specifically:

- A "senior foreign political figure" is a senior official in the executive, legislative, administrative, military or judicial branches of a foreign government (whether elected or not), a senior official of a major foreign political party, or a senior executive of a foreign government-owned corporation. In addition, a senior foreign political figure includes any corporation, business, or other entity that has been formed by, or for the benefit of, a senior foreign political figure.

- The "immediate family" of a senior foreign political figure typically includes the figure's parents, siblings, spouse, children, and in-laws.

- A "close associate" of a senior foreign political figure is a person who is widely and publicly known to maintain an unusually close relationship with the senior foreign political figure, and includes a person who is in a position to conduct substantial domestic and international financial transactions on behalf of the senior foreign political figure.

In Canada, according to FINTRAC "Politically Exposed Foreign Person Determination" document, a person is a politically exposed foreign person (PEFP) if the person holds or has ever held one of the following offices or positions in or on behalf of a foreign country:

- A head of state or government;

- A member of the executive council of government or member of a legislature;

- A deputy minister (or equivalent);

- An ambassador or an ambassador's attaché or counsellor;

- A military general (or higher rank);

- A president of a state-owned company or bank;

- A head of a government agency;

- A judge; or

- A leader or president of a political party in a legislature.

A person is also considered a PEFP if the person is a family member of an individual described above. In this context, a family member means one of the following:

- Mother or father;

- Child;

- Spouse or common-law partner;

- Spouse's or common-law partner's mother or father and

- Brother, sister, half-brother or half-sister (that is, any other child of the individual's mother or father).

Because of their position and the influence that they may hold, PEPs/PEFPs are vulnerable to ML/TF or other offences such as corruption and bribery. Both U.S. and Canada treat PEPs/PEFPs with heightened scrutiny using risk based approach.

Banks and financial institutions could get the list of PEPs from two sources: (1) open source – such as PEP information published by United Nations (UN), Interpol, U.S. Federal Bureau of Investigation (FBI), U.S. Central Intelligence Agency (CIA) and other international or national agencies; (2) third party commercial vendors – for example, Thomson Reuters World-Check, Dow Jones and many other PEP data providers.

Many financial institutions prefer to use a third party commercial PEP list and extend the PEP scanning to include domestic PEPs (i.e., individuals who are or have been entrusted domestically with prominent public functions or with prominent functions by state owned enterprises or international organizations) as well.

OSFI Consolidated List

Canada's legislative measures against terrorists, terrorist groups and other listed and sanctioned individuals and entities ("Designated Persons") are contained in various Canadian statutes and regulations. Subject to the Regulations Establishing a List of Entities made under subsection 83.05(1) of the Criminal Code, and/or the Regulations Implementing the United Nations Resolutions on the Suppression of Terrorism (RIUNRST) and/ or United Nations Al-Qaida and Taliban Regulations (UNAQTR), the Office of the Superintendent of Financial Institutions (OSFI) publishes on its web site (http://www.osfi-bsif.gc.ca/, retrieved on May 1, 2016) the up-to-date "OSFI Consolidated List" which is developed by the Department of Foreign Affairs and International Trade (DFAIT) and modified by the addition of names provided by Public Safety Canada to help institutions comply with specific regulatory measures in Canada.

The OSFI Consolidated Lists are in Excel (.xls) or text (.txt) format.

UN List and other watch-lists

The UN Consolidated Sanctions List includes all individuals and entities subject to sanctions measures imposed by the UN Security Council.

Consolidated United Nations Security Council Sanctions Lists are in Portable Document Format (PDF) (.pdf) or XML (.xml) or HyperText Markup Language (HTML) (.htm) format.

There are many other watch-lists available in the market, and financial institutions can create their own black lists for "bad guys" and white lists for "good guys". White lists are typically used for reducing false positives in the watch-list screening. Please see the Appendix A for further details.

The stripping and manipulation of identifying information on wire transfers and other financial messages, is designed to circumvent conventional watch-list screening controls. There is a so-called "fingerprinting" approach in some watch-list screening software packages which identifies wire transactions by matching its attributes to previously blocked wire transactions. When a regular wire transaction is blocked by an anti-stripping enabled (real-time transaction related) watch-list screening solution, the unalterable parts of the transaction's information (such as currency, amount, originator, beneficiary bank etc.) will be stored in a database and captured as a unique "fingerprint". When a stripped transaction enters the watch-list screening solution, its fingerprint can be calculated and if it matches any of those in the database, the transaction will be blocked, even though its identifying information might seem legitimate.

Society for Worldwide Interbank Financial Telecommunication (SWIFT) is a global member-owned cooperative and the world's leading provider of secure financial messaging services. SWIFT has developed KYC solutions (such as the KYC Registry and Sanctions Screening service) for SWIFT based transactions.

ADVERSE MEDIA

Adverse media is also known as negative news or negative media.

In our information overload age, every day around the world, there are societal scale media reports either in printed, electronic, radio or television formats in a variety of languages and with different level of detail depending on the visibility, sensitivity, scope and impact of the events being reported. In AML domain, more and more financial institutions are starting to use negative news as a helpful source of information when conducting EDD. But to find trustworthy/reliable context-based adverse media reference sources is not a trivial job, if not possible. The good news is more and more third party vendors now provide aggregated adverse media screening platforms, for example, solutions provided by LexisNexis WorldCompliance and Dow Jones Factiva.

Typically, aggregated adverse media sources provided by third party data aggregators allow users to perform name/attribute searches against named subjects online (or possibly in a batch mode) in multiple languages with unstructured/structured, dynamic and high frequency reference data.

TRANSACTION MONITORING

An ongoing monitoring process is used to assess activities for all customers with emphasis on customers and activities with the highest risks. According to U.S. FFIEC BSA/AML Examination Manual, "the sophistication of monitoring systems should be dictated by the bank's risk profile, with particular emphasis on the composition of higher-risk products, services, customers, entities, and geographies." And Canadian FINTRAC guidelines provide the similar principle.

DYNAMIC RISK RATING AND DUE DILIGENCE

To accommodate risk based approach, most leading AML information systems in the market support dynamic risk rating and risk based due diligence. That is, the AML information systems could generate/update risk profile at any point in the customer/account lifecycle:

- Support CDD at customer onboarding/account opening (for example, to import the expected behavior of each new customer or account, as obtained during customer onboarding/account opening)

- Support periodic updates/re-verification of KYC information on a risk-sensitive basis

A dynamic risk profile for a customer (an individual or a business entity) could be built using the dynamic risk rating and due diligence module. And an example is given below:

Individual
Date of birth (DoB)/Age range
Citizenship
Country of residence
Associates
Occupation
Geographic risk
Access to funds/Source of funds
High value assets
Legal events
Negative news
High-risk products and services
Expected behaviors (e.g., with respect to accounts and transactions)
Business Entity
Date of business establishment
Country of incorporation
Country of operation
Associates
Nature of business/Industry
Geographic risk
Access to funds/Source of funds
Business model/validity
Legal events
Negative news
High-risk products and services
Expected behaviors (e.g., with respect to accounts and transactions)

Table-3-1 A Sample of Customer Risk Profile

A risk profile could be quantified by assigning risk scores to underlined risks and then summing all the risk scores for the profile. A well-defined risk category would classify customers into different risk groups (e.g., 0 – 49 low, 50 – 79 medium, 80 – 100 high).

In turn, the risk insights provided by dynamic risk rating and due diligence help to guide financial institutions toward customers who may require heightened scrutiny or monitoring.

UNUSUAL ACTIVITY DETECTION

Most leading AML information systems in the market support two types of unusual activity detection:

- Rules-based monitoring/detection (e.g., system-developed or management-established "rules", such as a transaction greater than $10,000)

- Behavior-based monitoring/detection (e.g., frequent changes of address for a given customer)

Two examples below illustrate how a transaction monitoring module could be used to detect unusual activity:

Typologies	Rules/Behaviors
Structuring (also known as (AKA) Smurfing)	Structuring transactions (e.g., by paring down a more than $10,000 chunk of cash into smaller pieces, for example, around $7,000 or $9,000, and depositing them at different branches or in different accounts) to evade regulatory reporting and certain record keeping requirements can result in civil and criminal penalties. Detection rules (for a given customer): Rule 1a – all currency credit transactions >= $7,000 and < $10,000 of all accounts where the customer is the owner (or one of the owners) within a calendar day (or 24 hours) period; Rule 1b – all currency debit transactions >= $7,000 and < $10,000 of all accounts where the customer is the owner (or one of the owners) within a calendar day (or 24 hours) period; Rule 2 – if the accumulated value in (1a) or (1b) > $10,000, then an alert is generated.

Remote Deposit Capture (RDC)	In broad terms, RDC allows a bank's customers to scan a check or monetary instrument (MI), and then transmit the scanned or digitized image to the financial institution. RDC may expose banks to various risks, e.g., sequentially numbered, or physically altered documents, particularly money orders and traveler's checks, may be more difficult to detect when submitted by RDC (even in a foreign country) and not inspected by a qualified person. Detection behaviors (for a given customer): At any given day, if one performs a RDC transaction (with any monetary value) into an account associated with the customer, then an alert is generated.

Table-3-2 Samples of Structuring and Remote Deposit Capture

AML investigators could find some further or "hidden" relationships in a transaction monitoring module by reviewing shared pieces of information about customers, accounts, transactions and etc. within a financial institution, and most leading AML information systems in the market have sophisticated (typically with visual interfaces) network analysis modules.

NETWORK ANALYSIS

Network analysis is also called link analysis, which is a technique to explore associations among a large number of objects of same or different types with or without time dimension. In the AML domain, these objects might include involved parties/people, business entities, accounts, transactions, or events.

Visual representation of patterns or correlations between involved parties/people, business entities, accounts, transactions, or events can become one of the main exploratory techniques.

Typologies	Network/Link Analysis
"Hidden" relationships to account, transaction chains and "funnel account" suspect	Structuring of currency deposits into an account in one geographic area, with the funds subsequently withdrawn in a different geographic region with little time elapsing between deposit and withdrawal. This is usually known as "funnel account" or "interstate cash" activity in U.S. If John Doe is a suspect (or a known subject) of a funnel account (Account 1), then investigators might be able to find more "hidden" relationships by using network/ link analysis: Assume Account 2 is owned by Jean Doe and Account 1 shares a piece of information such as a phone number, address, or beneficiary in common with Account 2. Assume Account 3 is owned by another person (other than John Doe and Jean Doe) and Account 2 shares a different piece of data with Account 3 (say, both of the owner of Account 2 and Account 3 are beneficial owners of a business). By continuing this kind network/link analysis, investigators might be able to find a chain of involved parties, accounts and transactions that ultimately is linked to the "funnel account" suspect (or a known subject) John Doe.

Table-3-3 A Sample of Network Analysis

A financial institution could use network analysis (combining with other software modules) to gain further insights beyond KYC (know your

40

customer: understand who the customers are and what they do throughout the relationship with them), such as[14]

- KTYC – know the transactions of your customers: understand the transactions of the customer and have systems in place to spot any irregularities or suspicious activity.

- KCYC – know the customers of the customer: this extra level of understanding of the customers activities allows for an extra level of the KYC process.

- KYPB – know your partners in business: understand those partners the financial institution work with to avoid that indirectly the financial institution will be involved in unwanted activities.

- KYE – know your employees: criminal organizations need employees in the financial service industry to support them with illegal activities.

PEER GROUP ANALYSIS

The Peer Group Analysis uses statistical calculations to identify extreme deviations, generating alerts only when a customer's or an account's behavior is significantly different from others in the peer groups. Typically outliers could be detected both above and below expected behavior.

To use peer group analysis effectively, peer groups need to be well defined first. And there are few factors to consider for the definition of peer groups:

- A peer group is a group of objects (say, accounts, customers, etc.) that have similar attributes (say account type, age range, country of residence, industry code such as North American Industry

---

[14]   KTYC, KCYC, KYPB, KYE were coined by Jos de Wit in "A risk-based approach to AML: A controversy between financial institutions and regulators", Journal of Financial Regulation and Compliance, Vol. 15 No. 2, pp. 156 - 165, 2007

Classification System (NAICS) code, etc.) so that the comparison is between apples to apples, not apples to oranges.

- Due to the nature of statistical calculations (based on 'standard score', AKA Z-score[15]) for peer group profiling and scoring, the sizes of the peer groups members should be reasonably large (in other words, the size of a peer group will give a good representation of what expected behavior would be within the group).

- A behavior is available (i.e., could be well defined) for comparison within a peer group (e.g., cash transaction behavior).

- The to-be-compared object (account or customer) is a member of the peer group by definition.

[15] Allan G. Bluman, "Elementary Statistics: A Step by Step Approach (7th edition)", McGraw-Hill Higher Education, April, 2010

Typologies	Peer Group Analysis
Business entity in domestic higher-risk locations with unusual cash deposit transaction activity	Assume a bank has a good size of business customers in domestic higher-risk locations. In U.S., domestic higher-risk geographic locations include[16]: • High Intensity Drug Trafficking Areas (HIDTA) • High Intensity Financial Crime Areas (HIFCA) In Canada, FINTRAC (using big cities as samples) provides information sources of domestic high crime rate areas in the "Guidance on the Risk-Based Approach to Combatting Money laundering and Terrorist Financing" document. For a given domestic higher-risk geographic location, peer groups are defined using industry codes - NAICS Codes. Then the mean, standard deviation and cash deposit profile could be calculated daily for a peer group. If Acme Corporation is a customer of the bank (and is classified as a member of a peer group) and its cash deposit amount is beyond a threshold (say, $5,000) for a given day and the z-score is beyond a threshold (say, >= 3) against the group, then an alert is generated.

Table-3-4 A Sample of Peer Group Analysis

If peer groups are well defined and the data quality is good, then exceptionally high-quality alerts can be generated by leveraging peer group analysis.

---

[16] The lists of designated U.S. HIDTAs and HIFCAs are available at http://www.occ.gov/topics/compliance-bsa/bsa/law-enforcement-resources/index-law-enforcement-resources.html (retrieved on May 1, 2016)

CASE MANAGEMENT AND WORKFLOW

With an alert generated or an unusual transaction detected, the investigators need to begin the investigations. And financial institutions need an efficient workflow and case management solution enabling compliance staff to prioritize, perform and manage the investigations.

The following is a non-exhaustive list of features in a typical Workflow and Case Management module:

- Investigation tools to investigate alerts and/or suspicious activities (linking to customers, accounts, transactions, events, etc.)

- Built-in configurable workflow to route alerts/cases to specific investigators/reviewers, support (potentially automated) standard compliance procedures and facilitate team collaboration as well as enable segregation of duties (SoD), AKA separation of duties

- Dissemination of AML policies and procedures

- Life cycle case management (case creation/opening, prioritizing, investigations, updating/linking, closing/archiving, reporting, etc.)

- Record management for the investigations (the records/evidences and supporting documents have been captured and stored for alerts, cases and/or reports)

- Reporting capabilities (built-in, customized and/or ad hoc reports)

- Audit trails/logs of all actions taken and reports filed with the complete alert/case/report history

In certain cases, regulatory reports (CTR/LCTR, SAR/STR) need to be filed to FinCEN (in U.S.) or FINTRAC (in Canada) after evidences and supporting documents have been captured.

CTR/LCTR AND SAR/STR REPORTING

In U.S., a bank must electronically file a Currency Transaction Report (CTR) for each transaction in currency (deposit, withdrawal, exchange, or other payment or transfer) of more than $10,000 by, through, or to the bank.

Also banks, bank holding companies, and their subsidiaries are required by federal regulations to file a Suspicious Activity Report (SAR) with respect to:

- Criminal violations involving insider abuse in any amount.

- Criminal violations aggregating $5,000 or more when a suspect can be identified.

- Criminal violations aggregating $25,000 or more regardless of a potential suspect.

- Transactions conducted or attempted by, at, or through the bank (or an affiliate) and aggregating $5,000 or more, if the bank or affiliate knows, suspects, or has reason to suspect that the transaction:

  - May involve potential money laundering or other illegal activity (e.g., terrorist financing).

  - Is designed to evade the BSA or its implementing regulations.

  - Has no business or apparent lawful purpose or is not the type of transaction that the particular customer would normally be expected to engage in, and the bank knows of no reasonable explanation for the transaction after examining the available facts, including the background and possible purpose of the transaction.

In Canada, a bank or a reporting entity has to file a Large Cash Transaction Report (LCTR) to FINTRAC electronically or by paper in the following situations:

- The bank or the reporting entity receives an amount of $10,000 or more in cash in the course of a single transaction; or

- The bank or the reporting entity receives two or more cash amounts of less than $10,000 that total $10,000 or more (24-hour rule).

And a bank or a reporting entity has to file a Suspicious Transaction Report (STR) to FINTRAC electronically or by paper with respect to STR requirements specified in "Guideline 3: Submitting Suspicious Transactions Reports to FINTRAC".

Although both FinCEN and FINTRAC have their respective online filing system (the Bank Secrecy Act (BSA) E-Filing System for FinCEN and the F2R for FINTRAC) to allow a reporting entity to file a report manually, the benefits to use a transaction monitoring platform built-in regulatory reporting features are as follows:

- Automated data populating and report filing

- Batch mode submission

- Case management and workflow integration

- Data/information validation (data stored in the system against the reporting requirements)

- Segregation of duties (SoD) enablement

- Secure connection to FinCEN or FINTRAC

- Acknowledgement recording

- Refiling (in some situations)

- Reporting activity logging (audit trails)

By leveraging the reporting module in an AML platform, financial institutions could improve the efficiency and effectiveness of compliance programs.

Please also note that the reporting module in an AML platform might support other regulatory reports, such as FinCEN Form 105 Report of International Currency or Monetary Instruments (CMIR), FinCEN Form 114 Report of Foreign Bank and Financial Accounts (FBAR) and FinCEN Form 110 Designation of Exempt Person (DOEP) in the United States.

OTHER MODULES AND INTERFACES

In addition to the modules that have been discussed in previous sections, there are more modules, utilities and/or interfaces available in leading AML software.

The following is a non-exhaustive list of extra modules, utilities and/or interfaces:

- Data importer/loader

- Data exporter (e.g., to support alert/case/report data exporting)

- Network ID/Lightweight Directory Access Protocol (LDAP) integration to support the Single Sign-On (SSO)

- Role based user/permission management

- Systems (batch) job/task scheduler

- Dashboard

- Systems administration module (including system configuration)

- Interfaces to external systems (such as web services, application-programming interfaces (APIs))

- Real-time or near real-time transaction message scanning

In summary, AML information systems are used to meet the regulatory requirements for financial institutions to prevent or report money laundering activities. Essentially the systems capture, track, detect and report the movement of key elements in money laundering related activities:

- Involved parties (people flow)

- Transactions (money flow)

- Goods and services (logistics flow)

- Data exchanges and records (information flow)

Chapter 4

Unified Project Management and Implementation Framework

"In preparing for battle, I have always found that plans are useless but planning is indispensable."

— Dwight D. Eisenhower

IMPLEMENTATION CHALLENGES

Recent industry research and surveys, in North America and around the world, have revealed many challenges of AML information systems implementation.

SOME AML SURVEY RESULTS

In June 2015, Grant Thornton LLP published "Canada's compliance officers speak out", a report based on a survey of over 300 compliance officers in Canadian entities regulated by the Proceeds of Crime (Money Laundering) and Terrorist Financing Act (PCMLTFA). Some AML information systems related highlights from the report are:

- Respondents say they most frequently rely on their frontline staff to identify potentially suspicious activity. The next most important source of this information is compliance staff, with automated system monitoring falling into the last place.

- While a majority of companies (61%) rely on automated systems to manage record keeping, over 22% still use a manual, paper-based system. Only 57% have moved to automated transaction monitoring systems, while 23% perform manual reviews and 17% rely on systems like Microsoft Office Excel application.

Other global based AML surveys have revealed similar and extra AML information systems related challenges.

In February 2014, KPMG published "Global Anti-Money Laundering Survey 2014" with 317 survey participants from top global banks in 48 countries.

Some AML information systems related key headlines in KPMG's 2014 survey report are:

- Sanctions compliance remains a challenge as new issues emerge. 75% of respondents now use MT 202 COV SWIFT[17], but only 52% of respondents indicated that in every instance where an MT 202 COV lacked required information, it would be rejected.

- Transaction monitoring systems continue to represent the greatest area of AML spending, while satisfaction with these systems has declined with an average score of 3.42 out of 5 with regards to efficiency and effectiveness.

In March 2015, the "2015 Global Anti-Money Laundering Survey" of 1,118 AML professionals conducted by Dow Jones Risk & Compliance in conjunction with the Association of Certified Anti-Money Laundering Specialists (ACAMS) was released. And the

---

[17] Please refer to Appendix B. about the details of Cover Payments and SWIFT Message Type (MT) 202 COV.

survey results exhibited the following AML information systems related findings:

- Shortages of trained staff and technology concerns have become more widespread challenges.

  ◦ Insufficient or outdated technology - technology concerns are mentioned by 31% of respondents

  ◦ Too many false positive screening results - one-third of respondents report 75% or more of their Client Screening alerts are false positives.

- Data accuracy is the single "most important" factor in choosing AML data providers.

- More than 85% of respondents work in companies with client-screening technology solutions in place.

- Over 60% of respondents report their companies have "cleansed" customer data in the past six months.

- About 85% expect internal lists to be updated within 24 hours of changes to sanctioned/official lists.

From August 31, 2015 to September 14, 2015, LexisNexis and ACAMS conducted a joint research study to examine how the AML community is managing their customer Enhanced Due Diligence (EDD) and AML Risk Assessment processes. In total, over 800 financial services compliance professionals responded. In December 2015, LexisNexis Risk Solutions published the survey report "Current Industry Perspectives into Anti-Money Laundering Risk Management and Due Diligence". The AML information systems related hot topics in the survey results are:

- Bad data undermines compliance - Respondents stated they face many challenges in collecting the data they need to conduct thorough due diligence processes and maintain compliance with regulations. The data deficit is further compounded by a lack of confidence in the quality of the data collected from or provided by the end customer during onboarding.

- Customer reluctance to share information - A growing number of customers who are unwilling to share personally identifiable information (PII) that is needed to complete due diligence. In addition, survey respondents have a lack of confidence in the information customers do willingly share, with just 34% of respondents stating they find customer-provided statements of expected activity to be accurate.

LexisNexis survey report also indicated information technology (IT) infrastructure is one of greatest challenges identified in addition to the lack of readily accessible customer data, poor quality of available data, too many false-positives and growing volume of data.

LESSONS LEARNED FROM OTHERS

In addition to the input and feedback from industry research and surveys, there are many lessons learned in the trenches about information systems implementation projects (e.g., references [*33 - 36*]) with respect to challenges and opportunities:

- Unreasonable expectations (from management or other stakeholders)

- Lack of senior management support

- Lack of business end-user involvement

- Unclear business objectives and improperly identified requirements

- Insufficient, inefficient and ineffective communication (internally and externally)

- Lack of project management expertise/methodology and skilled project resources

- Lack of execution capacity and capability

- Lack of mature organizational processes such as governance models and operational processes

- Too many data related issues (availability, quality, integrity and etc.)

- Underestimated complexity of IT infrastructure, systems and architecture

- Over-customization of commercial off-the-shelf (COTS) packages

- Insufficient Quality Assurance (QA) testing

- Many other implementation challenges and opportunities

STAKEHOLDERS AND GOVERNANCE MODEL

To address AML information systems implementation challenges, the very first thing could and should be done is a stakeholder (persons, groups, organizations or government bodies who affect or can be affected by the AML information systems implementation) analysis for a financial institution.

STAKEHOLDER ANALYSIS

A sample high-level stakeholder analysis is summarized as follows (please note that for simplicity's sake, only one single jurisdiction AML information systems implementation situation is illustrated here):

Stakeholder	Roles and Responsibilities
The board of directors (BOD)	Overarching responsibility for AML/CFT or AML/ATF compliance, including but not limited to compliance governance model (and the BSA/AML compliance program must be written, approved by the board of directors).

Chief Compliance Officer (CCO)/ Chief AML Officer (CAMLO)	Overall accountability for the AML/CFT or AML/ATF policy, together with the responsibility for ongoing oversight and monitoring of the fulfilment of all AML/CFT or AML/ATF duties with the policy.
Senior management	The responsibility for ensuring the day-to-day AML/CFT or AML/ATF compliance with the policy and local regulatory requirements is assigned as well as adequate procedures and accountabilities are developed and implemented and appropriate resources are made available to execute them properly.
LOB/business unit management	The responsibility for working with the pertinent CCO/CAMLO to identify key control functions and develop and implement appropriate procedures in their respective work areas consistent with the AML compliance program, the applicable regulatory requirements and the risk profile of the business unit; ensuring appropriate employee awareness and training programs are developed and delivered consistent with the money laundering risk profile of the business unit.
AML Compliance Program Coordinator/ Manager	The responsibility for performing duties as assigned by the CCO/CAMLO; maintaining the process models and performing the role of business owner of the AML/CFT or AML/ATF information systems; and managing the reporting unit which performs a variety of functions under the AML program, e.g. supports ongoing watch list scans, performs various administrative functions related to the AML information systems, and completes various AML related reports.

Investigators	The responsibility for conducting a preliminary investigation and evaluation of unusual activities; reporting suspected cases of money laundering or terrorist financing to the CCO/CAMLO for further evaluation and resulting action; documenting investigation results and retaining records in accordance with regulatory requirements and the AML compliance program; working with CCO/CAMLO to conduct post investigations and help strengthen controls to prevent money laundering; and assisting in delivering training under the AML training program.
Legal department	The responsibility for monitoring, identifying and interpreting legislative and industry developments related to AML/CFT or AML/ATF obligations and trends; and communicating those developments, and where appropriate, recommending associated changes and possible strategy to the AML compliance program; providing necessary legal services and support to the AML compliance program as may be required.
Procurement department	The responsibility for the acquisition of goods and services as well as service providers in support of AML compliance program.
Finance department	The responsibility for supporting the delivery of AML compliance program with financial planning, implementation budgeting as may be required.

Human Resources (HR) department	The responsibility for performing due diligence and suitability reviews associated with the recruitment of new employees, and existing employees transferring into key roles under the AML compliance program; conducting initial orientation of new employees, including the AML/CFT or AML/ATF policy; as well as carrying out the assessment, determination and disposition of any alleged breach of the financial institution's policy by an employee, including any disciplinary action to be taken or termination of employment.
Internal Audit Services	The responsibility for reviewing the policies and procedures, the risk assessments and the training programs independently for the purpose of testing their effectiveness and efficiency; advising on AML risk management best practices.
IT/Information Systems (IS) infrastructure group	The responsibility for providing infrastructure related support with respect to the development and administration of the various information systems and applications utilized under a financial institution's AML compliance program.
IT/IS application support group	The responsibility for providing application related support (such as steady state and prioritized items - day to day operations of applications, break/fix solutions and small enhancement delivery) with respect to the development and administration of the various information systems and applications utilized under a financial institution's AML compliance program.
IT/IS data services group	The responsibility for providing data related support (such as integrated data repository or data hub) with respect to the development and administration of the various information systems and applications utilized under a financial institution's AML compliance program.

IT/IS QA group	The responsibility for performing quality assurance and testing management for various information systems and applications utilized under a financial institution's AML compliance program, including but not limited to the involvement of the enterprise data governance and ongoing data quality improvements and enhancements.
Information Security (InfoSec) risk management group	The responsibility for providing advisory services and oversighting information services risk disciplines including but not limited to Information Security (InfoSec), Information Services Risk, Information Audit & SOX Compliance, Information Privacy and Business Continuity.
IT/IS Help Desk	The responsibility for routing and handling the application access/security permission for various information systems and applications utilized under a financial institution's AML compliance program.
Financial institution's employees	The responsibility for adhering to the policies and procedures established under the AML/CFT or AML/ATF Program.
Project Management Office (PMO)	The responsibility for enabling a financial institution to achieve its business objectives, by ensuring project success through the facilitation and influencing of project management best practices, in partnership with the financial institution's project teams.
Shareholders and general public	The shareholders of a financial institution and general public are impacted by the institution's AML compliance results positively or negatively. Also the shareholders of a financial institution and general public may influence the institution's compliance context.

External service providers/partners	The responsibility for providing the value-added services to the financial institution, including but not limited to business services (such as wire transfer service), compliance outsourcing, IT infrastructure, software packages and data services for the AML compliance program.
External audit services	The responsibility for performing similar functions that internal audit services group usually do but often bringing in advising and consulting work that could rationalize or enhance a financial institution's AML program.
Regulatory examiners/ inspectors	The responsibility for carrying out AML compliance examinations/inspections by representing regulators or other authorities.
Regulators and/or other government bodies	The responsibility for reducing the extent to which it is possible for a regulated business to be used for a purpose connected with financial crime; maintaining confidence in the financial system; contributing to the protection and enhancement of stability of the financial system; securing the appropriate degree of protection for consumers; regulating foreign participation in the financial markets.

Table-4-1 Stakeholder Analysis

For an AML information systems implementation, after the stakeholder analysis (which usually is more specific and detailed than the sample one given above) is completed, then based upon the analysis the implementation governance model could be established accordingly.

IMPLEMENTATION GOVERNANCE

Different financial institutions have different organization context (due to various size, structure, nature and complexity of the organizations, different business models, compliance cultures and etc.), so they may need to employ different implementation governance models. A generic sample of implementation governance models is given below but "your mileage may vary".

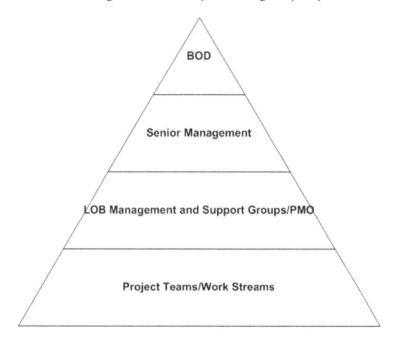

Figure-4-1 Implementation Governance (Internal)

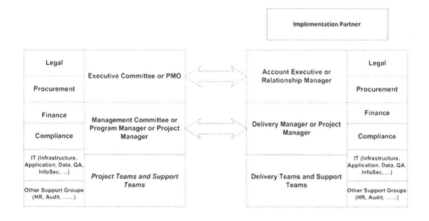

Figure-4-2 Implementation Governance (External)

With implementation governance model in place, the implementation planning could be started. Typically a financial institution's AML information systems implementation involves one-time project (a temporary endeavor undertaken to create a unique product, service or result) to deploy the systems and on-going maintenance and operations of the systems.

Work Breakdown Structure and Project Management Framework

For the project planning, the work breakdown structure (WBS) is a common yet powerful tool. A work breakdown structure is defined by the Project Management Institute (PMI) Project Management Body of Knowledge (PMBOK) as "a hierarchical decomposition of the total scope of work to be carried out by the project team to accomplish the project objectives and create the required deliverables."

The fundamental idea of WBS is to divide the implementation deliverables and project work into smaller, more manageable components.

WBS and Implementation Planning

In this section, a sample of simplified (without the labeling of dependencies, constraints, efforts and durations) high-level WBS is given based on the assumption that some commercial off-the-shelf (COTS) packages (e.g., third party KYC data and screening software, third party transaction monitoring software) are used for the AML information systems implementation.

WBS Code	Description
1.0	**Implementation Engagement and Project Management**
1.1	Project charter[18]
1.2	Initial project engagement (including but not limited to initial project resource allocation)
1.3	Initial project planning
1.4	Approved project plan
1.5	Project change management

---

[18] Some organizations have a project gating process and some organizations may only require a project charter or Statement of Work (SOW).

2.0	**Pre-RFP (Request for Proposal) Activities**
2.1	Current state, future state and gap analysis
2.2	Market research (on vendors, products and technologies in current market)
2.3	Needs, wants and desires identification as well as essential implementation business/functional/non-functional requirements gathering
2.4	List of potential vendors
2.5	Evaluation criteria creation as well as evaluation and selection procedure design
3.0	**RFP Activities**
3.1	RFP creation
3.2	RFP distribution to potential vendors
3.3	Questions and Answers (Q & As) to all potential vendors
3.4	Best and Final Offers (BAFO) from the potential vendors (bidders)
4.0	**Post-RFP Activities and Vendor Selection**
4.1	Proposals evaluation
4.2	Short list of vendors
4.3	Presentation review for each shortlisted vendor as well as Questions and Answers with shortlisted vendors
4.4	"Proof of Concept" (PoC) requirements gathering and distribution to shortlisted vendors
4.5	Shortlisted vendor's PoC demos
4.6	Detailed discussions with shortlisted vendors with respect to implementation pain points and possible solutions
4.7	Vendor comparison, ranking and selection (1st choice and 2nd choice)
4.8	Reference check for selected vendor(s)
4.9	Contract negotiation
4.10	Sign-off on the Master Service Agreement (MSA)/Service Level Agreement (SLA) with the winning vendor(s)
5.0	**Implementation Business Requirements Refinement**
5.1	Selected vendor's infrastructure, software and data requirements
5.2	Initial sizing of required infrastructure (servers, network storage, etc.), software packages (database software, application software, etc.) and data (volume, frequency, growth rate, data input format etc.) per vendor's requirements
5.3	Vendor's workshop

5.4	Implementation business/functional/non-functional requirements refinement
5.5	Sign-off on the agreed requirements and requirements traceability matrix (RTM)
5.6	Vendor's solution documents and vendor's proposed project plan or implementation plan
5.7	Project planning update and integration (with necessary project change management)
5.8	Extra project resource allocation
6.0	**Analysis, Specifications and Design of Systems**
6.1	Detailed infrastructure related analysis (including but not limited to capacity planning and access controls)
6.2	Detailed application related analysis (including but not limited to systems interfaces such as web services to wire or ACH transaction systems)
6.3	Detailed data related analysis (including but not limited to source data Extract, Transform and Load (ETL) process)
6.4	Detailed QA planning and analysis
6.5	Other systems related analysis (including but not limited to information risk assessment, information audit, Business Continuity Planning (BCP) and Disaster Recovery Planning (DRP) analysis)
6.6	Infrastructure related specifications and architecture design
6.7	Application related specifications and design
6.8	Data related specifications (including but not limited to data mapping specifications, batch process) and design
6.9	QA related documentation (including but not limited to test plan and test strategy) and design (including but not limited to test cases, test scripts, test data sets)
6.10	Other systems related specifications and design
7.0	**Build (Development)**
7.1	Vendor's deployment packages (with unit test) creation and documents
7.2	Necessary infrastructure components purchase and (with unit test) creation
7.3	Necessary application components (with unit test) creation
7.4	Necessary source data hub and ETL process (with unit test) creation

7.5	Necessary QA preparation (including but not limited to QA scripts creation)
7.6	Other necessary systems components (with unit test) creation (including but not limited to access control list and etc.)
8.0	**System Integration Test** (SIT)
8.1	SIT environment creation
8.2	Deployment of vendor's packages (including but not limited to the configuration) in SIT environment
8.3	Deployment of necessary application components in SIT environment
8.4	Deployment of necessary data components (source data hub, ETL process and etc.) in SIT environment
8.5	Deployment of other necessary systems components in SIT environment
8.6	Test data creation and loading (including but not limited to the data right sizing and possible data masking) in SIT environment
8.7	SIT execution
8.8	Support of SIT from all involved parties
8.9	Bug fixes, if any
8.10	Sign-off on the SIT testing
9.0	**User Acceptance Test (UAT) or Business Acceptance Test (BAT) or Client Acceptance Test** (CAT)
9.1	UAT environment creation
9.2	Deployment of vendor's packages (including but not limited to the configuration) in UAT environment
9.3	Deployment of necessary application components in UAT environment
9.4	Deployment of necessary data components (source data hub, ETL process and etc.) in UAT environment
9.5	Deployment of other necessary systems components in UAT environment
9.6	Production-like data loading (production data loading with adjustments for certain detection scenarios to fully cover all test cases)
9.7	UAT user training
9.8	UAT execution
9.9	Support of UAT from all involved parties
9.10	Bug fixes, if any

9.11	Detection scenario parameter tuning per business feedback
9.12	Sign-off on the UAT testing and tuning results
10.0	**Production Deployment**
10.1	Production deployment planning and preparation
10.2	Operational Readiness Testing
10.3	Production environment creation
10.4	Deployment of vendor's packages (including but not limited to the configuration) in production environment
10.5	Deployment of necessary application components in production environment
10.6	Deployment of necessary data components (source data hub, ETL process and etc.) in production environment
10.7	Deployment of other necessary systems components in production environment
10.8	Data loading or migration (for history data) in production environment
10.9	Support of production deployment from all involved parties
10.10	Post-Implementation Verification/Validation (PIV)
10.11	Any necessary adjustments per the PIV results
10.12	Go/No Go decision
10.13	DRP/BCP environment creation
10.14	End user training
10.15	Final project documentation
11.0	**Post Implementation Tasks**
11.1	Service Level Agreement (SLA) activation with vendors/ service provides
11.2	Operational Level Agreement (OLA) activation with internal groups
11.3	Production support during the warranty period by vendors/ service provides and internal groups
11.4	Knowledge transfer from the project team to on-going support team
11.5	Lessons learned from the implementation
11.6	Ongoing maintenance and operational tasks (including but not limited to profile building/updating, database backup/ restore and etc.)
11.7	Compliance performance metric/baseline creation
11.8	Calibration and enhancements

Table-4-2 A Sample of Work Breakdown Structure (WBS)

After AML COTS systems vendor(s) and/or service provider(s) are selected, the project manager and implementation team members need to put all the pieces together by consolidating all the WBS/proposed implementation plans into an "integrated master WBS/plan."

The implementation plan can then be derived by using the integrated master WBS and project management methodologies (the global project management standards and methodologies, such as PMBOK or ISO 21500:2012 "Guidance on Project Management" could be found in references [*37 - 40*]):

- Integrated master WBS → all the work required, and only the work required to complete the implementation successfully → project scope baseline → project scope management plan

- Integrated master WBS → schedule activities + sequencing and dependencies → project schedule baseline + milestones and critical paths → project schedule management plan

- Integrated master WBS → activity based costing (ABC) → project cost baseline and cost allocations → project cost management plan

- Integrated master WBS → test strategies, test plans, test cases, test data, test tools, test scripts, test environment → project quality management plan

- Integrated master WBS → organizational breakdown structure (OBS) + resource breakdown structure (RBS) + resource availability → responsibility assignment matrix (RAM) → project staffing management plan

- Integrated master WBS → When, Where, Who, What, Why and How to communicate → project communication management plan

- Integrated master WBS → risk breakdown structure (RBS) → risk register → project risk management plan

- Integrated master WBS → updated project procurement management plan

- Integrated master WBS → project financial plan + change management plan + project control plan + contract management plan + vendor relationship management plan + acceptance plan + ...

CHANGE MANAGEMENT

In today's ever changing environment, it is not surprising that there might be needs for a financial institution to modify business requirements or functional/non-functional requirements during the implementation cycle. The implementation team shouldn't manage ad hoc changes on the fly but rather follow disciplined project change management best practices. Typically the project manager and implementation team need to:

- Identify a change requirement

- Perform the impact analysis and possible solutions to the requested change

- Obtain the necessary approval from key stakeholders for the change

- Adjust the project plan baseline accordingly

- Communicate the change openly with all involved parties

- Manage the change through its implementation

- Ensure the change is deployed into production effectively as business expected

OTHER IMPLEMENTATION MANAGEMENT TOPICS

Depending on the nature and complexity of the AML information systems implementation as well as enterprise environmental factors, different financial institutions may have different considerations and approaches.

PHASED APPROACH

For certain financial institutions, a strategy of implementing AML information systems, business/compliance processes, etc. in a phased way makes perfect sense.

For example, if a financial institution scans the AML software market and finds out the best of breed vendors in KYC screening domain may not be the best ones in transaction monitoring domain (or vice versa), then the institution may choose two different third party vendors for the AML compliance program (one for KYC screening and another for transaction monitoring). And a phased approach could be to implement KYC screening systems and related business/compliance processes first (as phase 1) in the institution and then implement transaction monitoring systems and related business/compliance processes in the next phase (phase 2).

Also, in a global financial institution, it is common to implement procured (by a centralized procurement department) AML information systems in different jurisdictions in a phased way: U.S. Division implements first, Asia Division implements second, and so on so forth.

PROJECT VERSUS PROGRAM

According to PMI PMBOK, a program is defined as "a group of related projects, subprograms, and program activities managed in a coordinated way to obtain benefits not available from managing them individually".

For a big financial institution, such as a global systemically important bank (G-SIB) or a domestic systemically important bank (D-SIB), the AML information systems implementation program (instead of a single project) could bring important business benefits to the whole bank globally. Under the program (typically located at the institution's headquarter), there might be many projects, for example, each LOB has its own project: Retail Banking, Private Banking, Business Banking, Investments, and etc.

A work stream is defined in the Business Dictionary as "the progressive completion of tasks completed by different groups within a company which are required to finish a single project".

Within a project (e.g., Retail Banking AML information systems implementation) there might be multiple work streams such as wire and ACH work stream, credit card work stream, lending work stream and etc. that can cut across frontline, compliance and IT groups in the institution.

WATERFALL VERSUS AGILE

Traditional stages of a project resemble a waterfall:

Figure-4-3 Waterfall Methodology

While an agile methodology, e.g., Scrum, is an iterative, incremental and interactive agile software development framework for managing product development. A development team that uses Scrum, or some other agile methodologies, would approach the same development project as a series of very small projects called sprints. And working software package is released periodically in an iterative manner until the entire software product is complete.

Typically the final goals of an AML information systems implementation project are clearly defined, so the overall project is suitable to use the traditional waterfall methodology but a flexible approach that embraces both traditional and agile development principles (so called "Water-Agile-Fall", "Water-Scrum-Fall" etc.) could allow development teams to use whatever practices and techniques best meet the business needs. Many organizations use agile principles (e.g., Scrum communication techniques) in their day-to-day development but employ the traditional waterfall methodology for planning, budgeting or documenting the project's progress.

PROJECTS VERSUS OPERATIONS

The implementation of AML information systems in this book is not only including the one-time project to deploy the systems into the production environment but also including on-going maintenance and operations of the systems as well as the on-going compliance/business functioning.

There are many similarities between projects and operations, such as:

- Both are performed by people

- Both are constrained by limited resources

- Both should be planned, executed, and controlled

And there are many differences between projects and operations, such as:

Projects	Operations
Temporary (with a start date and an end date)	Ongoing
Output: Unique	Output: Repetitive
Purpose: Attain its objective and then terminate	Purpose: Sustain the business functions
A project concludes when its specific objectives have been attained	Operations adopt a new set of objectives and the work continues

Table-4-3 Projects vs. Operations

Many implementation pain points and challenges mentioned before (such as lack of senior management support; lack of business end-user involvement; lack of mature organizational processes; insufficient, inefficient and ineffective communication (internally and externally); lack of project management expertise and/or methodology) could be addressed or alleviated by applying thorough stakeholder analysis, proper governance models, open communications and project management best practices.

In the next chapter (Chapter 5), the main technical topics of both one-time project part and on-going maintenance and operations part of the implementation (especially the pain points often encountered) will be discussed in detail.

System Implementation Life Cycle

"A good idea is about ten percent and implementation and hard work, and luck is 90 percent."

— Guy Kawasaki

PRE-DEPLOYMENT

Before a financial institution starts the implementation of AML information systems, the key stakeholders in the institution need to think about many questions such as "where are we now?", "where are we going?", "how do we get there from here?" with respect to the AML compliance program and related information systems.

CURRENT STATE, FUTURE STATE AND GAP ANALYSIS

In this subsection, the "beneficial owner" topic is used to demonstrate an approach to how the current state, future state and gap analysis could be done by a U.S.[19] based bank's compliance program.

According to the U.S. FFIEC BSA/AML Examination Manual, a beneficial owner is an individual or a business "who has a level of control over, or entitlement to, the funds or assets in the account that, as a practical matter, enables the individual, directly or indirectly, to control, manage, or direct the account. The ability to fund the account or the entitlement to the funds of the account alone, however, without any corresponding authority to control, manage, or direct the account (such as in the case of a minor child beneficiary), does not cause the individual to be a beneficial owner."

And in August 2014, FinCEN released the Notice of Proposed Rulemaking (NPRM) about the "Beneficial Ownership Rule" which explored a definition of "beneficial owner" (a natural person, not another legal entity) with two independent components, referred to as "prongs" for financial institutions:

1. Ownership Prong - Each individual, if any, who, directly or indirectly, through any contract, arrangement, understanding, relationship or otherwise, owns 25 percent or more of the equity interests of a legal entity customer; and

2. Control Prong - An individual with significant responsibility to control, manage, or direct a legal entity customer, including

   (A) An executive officer or senior manager (e.g., a Chief Executive Officer, Chief Financial Officer, Chief Operating Officer, Managing Member, General Partner, President, Vice President, or Treasurer); or

---

[19] To align with international standards, Canada has escalated its beneficial ownership requirements for Reporting Entities effective on February 1, 2014. Please refer to FINTRAC "Policy Interpretations: Beneficial Ownership" for more details. And the U.S. FinCEN released the new beneficial ownership requirement of legal entity customers on May 6, 2016.

(B) Any other individual who regularly performs similar functions.

The key stakeholders of the AML compliance program in a U.S. based bank need to perform the current state, future state and gap analysis by evaluating the people, processes, technology and data (i.e., information) for the beneficial owner requirements:

People

- Where are we now? (i.e., current state) Among all internal three lines of defense and external partners/service providers, who are responsible for what for existing Customer Due Diligence requirements? Who are responsible for the special due diligence of existing (i.e., effective prior to May 11, 2016) "beneficial owner" requirements for private bank accounts and correspondent accounts for certain foreign financial institutions?

- Where are we going? (i.e., future state) If the FinCEN new beneficial ownership rule gets fulfilled in the future, who should be responsible for what among all internal three lines of defense and external partners/service providers?

- How do we get there from here? (i.e., gaps analysis and bridges/ approaches) The FinCEN new beneficial ownership rule has stated that CDD consists of at least the following four elements:

  1. Identifying and verifying the identity of customers (explicit in existing requirements);

  2. Identifying and verifying the identity of beneficial owners of legal entity customers (explicit in existing requirements for private bank accounts and correspondent accounts for certain foreign financial institutions);

  3. Understanding the nature and purpose of customer relationships (implicit in existing requirements); and,

4. Conducting ongoing monitoring to maintain and update customer information and to identify and report suspicious transactions (implicit in existing requirements)

Identifying natural persons who are beneficial owners and/or who have effective control may be difficult and tedious, if not impossible. If FinCEN new beneficial ownership rule gets fulfilled in the future, more human resources (people) are required in all three lines of defense for extra work load: customer-facing account/relationship managers, operation managers, compliance officers, investigators, risk managers, IT group members, auditors and etc.

Processes

- Current state – What are the current business, compliance and IT processes/controls with respect to existing "beneficial owner" requirements?

- Future state – If FinCEN new beneficial ownership rule gets fulfilled in the future, what would be the modified/enhanced or new business, compliance and IT processes/controls with respect to new "beneficial owner" requirements?

- Gaps and bridges/approaches – What are the gaps in terms of business, compliance and IT processes/controls (such as how to verify a natural person who meets "Control Prong") and what would be the process related approaches if FinCEN new beneficial ownership rule gets fulfilled in the future?

Technology

- Current state – What are the current IT infrastructure, applications and capacity to accommodate existing "beneficial owner" requirements?

- Future state – What are the impacts to IT infrastructure (such as the storage devices or servers), applications and capacity as well as what would be the enhanced/new IT infrastructure and solution requirements if FinCEN new beneficial ownership rule gets fulfilled in the future?

- Gaps and bridges/approaches – What are the gaps in terms of IT infrastructure and solutions (such as new third party data services) and what would be the technology approaches if FinCEN new beneficial ownership rule gets fulfilled in the future?

Data

- Current state – What kind of data is collected and updated as well as how the collected data is processed and used with respect to existing "beneficial owner" requirements?

- Future state – What would be the enhanced/new information that would be collected and processed if the FinCEN new beneficial ownership rule gets fulfilled in the future?

- Gaps and bridges/approaches – What kind of data elements that are not collected/processed today but required if the FinCEN new beneficial ownership rule gets fulfilled in the future? And what would be the approaches to gather, process and update the required (up-to-date) data if the FinCEN new beneficial ownership rule gets fulfilled in the future (e.g., to use "selfcertification" as a primary method or other methods)?

To collect and verify the complex structure information of a business entity could be cumbersome and third party data services (such as Dun & Bradstreet's Beneficial Ownership data service) might be helpful. For example, if one searches U.S. Securities and Exchange Commission (SEC) EDGAR (Electronic Data Gathering, Analysis, and Retrieval) system about archived Exhibit 21 data for "Valeant Pharmaceuticals International, Inc.", a multinational specialty drugs company, the result[20] indicated that

---

[20]   Archived (February 25, 2015) Exhibit 21 data for "Valeant Pharmaceuticals International, Inc." is available at
http://www.sec.gov/Archives/edgar/data/885590/000088559015000015/exhibit211.htm
(retrieved on May 1, 2016)

as of February 25, 2015, Valeant Pharmaceuticals International, Inc. had well over 200 subsidiaries worldwide. And it wouldn't be an easy task to identify and verify the natural persons who satisfy the Ownership Prong and Control Prong for the company.

AML Typologies and Models

After a thorough current state, future state and gap analysis, the key stakeholders of the AML information systems implementation need to consider what detection scenarios are required to be implemented and what are the parameters and threshold values/scores for each scenario.

For financial institutions, there is no "one-size fits all" solution to developing detection scenarios (AKA red flag scenarios) that need to be implemented since each institution has its own unique characteristics: size; ownership structure; nature, scope and complexity of operations; corporate strategy; risk appetite and profile; geographical locations and etc. But financial institutions could design and develop suitable detection scenarios by learning from many sources, such as:

- Typology reports published by regulators and international bodies (typologies work is the study of methods, techniques and trends of money laundering and terrorist financing), for example:

  - U.S. IRS examples of money laundering investigations and FinCEN SAR activity review – trends, tips & issues

  - Canadian FINTRAC typologies and trends reports

  - FATF methods and trends publications

- Built-in libraries of detection scenarios in AML information systems provided by vendors

- Knowledge sharing from peer financial institutions or industry organizations

And the key stakeholders of the AML information systems implementation in a financial institution need to make sure the conceptual soundness of developed detection scenarios:

- Are the coverage and capabilities of the developed detection scenarios in line with the risk profile of the institution?

- Are the coverage and capabilities of the developed detection scenarios for intended use?

- Are there any material gaps in the developed detection scenarios?

After detection scenarios are designed and developed, how to set up proper parameters, threshold values/scores for each scenario?

In April 2011, the U.S. Office of the Comptroller of the Currency (OCC) and Board of Governors of the Federal Reserve System (FRB) published "Supervisory Guidance on Model Risk Management" for banks on effective model risk management (the reference [46]) and the guidance imposed compliance requirements (including, but not limited to, AML compliance) to all banks.

What is a model and how models are related to an AML detection scenario and parameters, threshold values/scores of the detection scenario?

According to OCC/FRB guidance, the term model "refers to a quantitative method, system, or approach that applies statistical, economic, financial, or mathematical theories, techniques, and assumptions to process input data into quantitative estimates".

A model consists of three components:

- An information input component, which delivers assumptions and data to the model;

- A processing component, which transforms inputs into estimates;

- And a reporting component, which translates the estimates into useful business information.

Models are simplified representations of real-world relationships among observed characteristics, values, and events. Therefore an AML detection scenario or a collection of AML detection scenarios or even a component of AML software (such as a watch-list screen platform) could be viewed as a model and parameters, threshold values/scores of the detection scenarios are derived from input data and the institution's risk assessment:

- Parameters should be established based on internal, unique factors at the institution such as:

  ◦ Products, services and delivery channels;

  ◦ Geographic locations;

  ◦ Customer base and business relationships;

  ◦ Volume of higher risk customers and regulatory reports

  ◦ Other relevant and historical information

- Threshold values/scores are compliance driven and data driven based upon the unique characteristics of the institution. In other words, thresholds and scores should be set up based on the thorough quantitative and qualitative analysis.

It is often said that "the results are only as good as the (input) data available". The availability, completeness, quality, accuracy and integrity of data are the industry challenges that need to be addressed before the key implementation stakeholders even try to set up the threshold values/scores for detection scenarios. Thus more technical topics about the model development, implementation and use are postponed in later sections of the chapter after some data related topics are discussed.

BCBS 239 PRINCIPLES

In January 2013, the Basel Committee on Banking Supervision (BCBS) published document BCBS 239, "Principles for Effective Risk Data

Aggregation and Reporting" (also commonly known as RDARR principles), which has a set of guidelines to demand that the information banks use to drive decision-making captures all risks with appropriate accuracy and timeliness. Although at this moment the BCBS 239 pertains only to global systemically important banks (G-SIBs) and domestic systemically important banks (D-SIBs), its overarching principles set the foundation for the data management best practices for any bank.

Data management has a long history well before January 2013. For example, master data management (MDM) was and still is one of the best practices in enterprise data warehouse (EDW/DW) area and MDM comprises the governance, standards, processes, policies, and tools that consistently define and manage the critical data of an organization to provide a single point of reference. But BCBS 239 principles are intended to address a pervasive issue in the financial services industry that many banks lack the ability to identify and aggregate risk exposures quickly and accurately at the bank group level, across business lines and between legal entities. Please note that risk exposures are beyond but including money laundering risk which is a part of operational risk per international regulatory framework for banks, i.e., Basel framework.

In BCBS 239, there are 14 principles grouped into four categories:

Governance and Infrastructure	A bank should have in place a strong governance framework, risk data architecture and IT infrastructure. The board and senior management are called out to understand coverage and limitations.
Principle 1	Governance – A bank's risk data aggregation capabilities and risk reporting practices should be subject to strong governance arrangements consistent with other principles and guidance established by the Basel Committee on Banking Supervision (BCBS).

Principle 2	Data architecture and IT infrastructure – A bank should design, build and maintain data architecture and IT infrastructure which fully supports its risk data aggregation capabilities and risk reporting practices not only in normal times but also during times of stress or crisis, while still meeting the other Principles.
Risk Data Aggregation Capabilities	Banks must demonstrate the ability to generate accurate and reliable risk data in a timely manner even for ad hoc reports during a crisis or at the request of the regulator
Principle 3	Accuracy and Integrity – A bank should be able to generate accurate and reliable risk data to meet normal and stress/crisis reporting accuracy requirements. Data should be aggregated on a largely automated basis so as to minimize the probability of errors.
Principle 4	Completeness – A bank should be able to capture and aggregate all material risk data across the banking group. Data should be available by business line, legal entity, asset type, industry, region and other groupings, as relevant for the risk in question, that permit identifying and reporting risk exposures, concentrations and emerging risks.
Principle 5	Timeliness – A bank should be able to generate aggregate and up-to-date risk data in a timely manner while also meeting the principles relating to accuracy and integrity, completeness and adaptability. The precise timing will depend upon the nature and potential volatility of the risk being measured as well as its criticality to the overall risk profile of the bank. The precise timing will also depend on the bank-specific frequency requirements for risk management reporting, under both normal and stress/crisis situations, set based on the characteristics and overall risk profile of the bank.

Principle 6	Adaptability – A bank should be able to generate aggregate risk data to meet a broad range of on-demand, ad hoc risk management reporting requests, including requests during stress/crisis situations, requests due to changing internal needs and requests to meet supervisory queries.
Risk Reporting Practices	Ensuring the right information is accurately presented to the right people in a clear & useful manner at the right time.
Principle 7	Accuracy - Risk management reports should accurately and precisely convey aggregated risk data and reflect risk in an exact manner. Reports should be reconciled and validated.
Principle 8	Comprehensiveness - Risk management reports should cover all material risk areas within the organization. The depth and scope of these reports should be consistent with the size and complexity of the bank's operations and risk profile, as well as the requirements of the recipients.
Principle 9	Clarity and usefulness - Risk management reports should communicate information in a clear and concise manner. Reports should be easy to understand yet comprehensive enough to facilitate informed decision-making. Reports should include meaningful information tailored to the needs of the recipients.
Principle 10	Frequency – The board and senior management (or other recipients as appropriate) should set the frequency of risk management report production and distribution. Frequency requirements should reflect the needs of the recipients, the nature of the risk reported, and the speed, at which the risk can change, as well as the importance of reports in contributing to sound risk management and effective and efficient decision-making across the bank. The frequency of reports should be increased during times of stress/crisis.

Principle 11	Distribution - Risk management reports should be distributed to the relevant parties while ensuring confidentiality is maintained.
Supervisory Review, Tools and Co-Operation	The regulators should ensure they can evaluate & remediate compliance accurately and effectively.
Principle 12	Review - Supervisors should periodically review and evaluate a bank's compliance with the eleven Principles above.
Principle 13	Remedial actions and supervisory measures - Supervisors should have and use the appropriate tools and resources to require effective and timely remedial action by a bank to address deficiencies in its risk data aggregation capabilities and risk reporting practices. Supervisors should have the ability to use a range of tools, including the supervisory review process in BCBS "Enhancements to the Basel II framework".
Principle 14	Home/host cooperation - Supervisors should cooperate with relevant supervisors in other jurisdictions regarding the supervision and review of the Principles, and the implementation of any remedial action if necessary.

Table-5-1 BCBS 239 Principles

The rest of this section is focusing on the BCBS 239 "Risk Data Aggregation Capabilities" part principles and data required for an AML information systems implementation.

Data availability and lineage

The data elements that are required for AML compliance are customers, accounts, transactions, and other information (such as events, expected behaviors, non-financial activities etc.).

In a financial institution, the data for fundamental business operations may not be available or complete for various reasons:

- Customer – Customers are classified by different types in a bank: individuals and entities, there are many sub-types for entity-type customers (and corresponding beneficial owners). In the insurance world, customers are beyond the parties who purchased the insurance policies (e.g., policy owners, insured persons, beneficiaries etc.).

- Account – Accounts in a bank have many types: savings accounts, demand deposit accounts (DDAs), money market deposit accounts (MMDAs), certificates of deposit (CDs) in U.S./guaranteed investment certificates (GICs) in Canada etc. In the investment trading world, accounts typically have extra information: positions, market values etc.

- Transaction – The requirements for collecting necessary AML compliance related data are different for different types of financial transactions (cash deposits/withdrawals, debit card transactions, credit card transactions, automated teller machine (ATM)/automated banking machine (ABM) transactions etc.), for example, wire or ACH transactions require extra transaction related information (please see Appendix B. for technical details).

Data lineage is defined as a data life cycle that includes the data's origins and where it moves over time. So, as the first item of "know your data (KYD)" exercise, the implementation team members need to find the availability of each required data element for the implementation and start to build the inventory/taxonomy of authoritative (or "golden version" of) source data systems as well as the data lineage within the institution.

If the data is not available or the information is not complete for a required data element, then implementation team members could and should follow BCBS 239 principles to request the corresponding LOBs to collect or remediate the data.

Data standardization, quality, accuracy and integrity

One important aspect to address common data quality, accuracy and integrity issues is to standardize the data across the whole institution and/ or purchased commercial industry data. By following the guiding principles specified in BCBS 239, a financial institution could benefit from the concept of the shared service and provision of standards. For example, any data used to categorize other data, or for relating data to information beyond the boundaries of the enterprise is so called reference data. And for AML compliance purpose, many data elements are in the "reference data" category:

- Countries (and dependent territories), which could and should be standardized by using ISO 3166 country codes (such as ISO 3166-1 alpha-2 for two-letter country codes, ISO 3166-1 alpha-3 for three-letter country codes, ISO 3166-1 numeric for three-digit country codes)

- States in U.S. or Provinces in Canada, which could and should be standardized by using American National Standards Institute (ANSI) State Codes or Canada Post Province/Territory Codes

- Names of individual type customers (or individual type parties in general) should be able to split into (First name, Middle name, Last name) format properly

- Currencies could and should be standardized by using ISO 4217 Currency (alphabetic or numeric) Codes

- Some account or transaction related data elements should follow the corresponding standards or specifications: e.g., American Bankers Association numbers (AKA ABA routing numbers or ABA routing transfer numbers (ABA RTN)), SWIFT Business Identifier Codes (BICs, ISO 9362), International Bank Account Numbers (IBANs)

- Industry codes should be standardized by using NAICS codes or Standard Industrial Classification (SIC) codes

- Certain types of reference data (such as customer status, account types, transaction codes, occupation codes etc.) should be consolidated and standardized by using codes that are generally acceptable across LOBs within the institution, e.g., Standard Occupational Classification (SOC) codes in U.S. and National Occupational Classification (NOC) codes in Canada could be used for occupations

- Address (street address, city, state/province, zip/postal code) data is important information in AML compliance. For existing source systems, if possible, the institution could use homegrown or third party vendor's software packages to remediate the inaccurate or bad address data; for brand new source systems or system components (e.g., a new component to collect beneficial ownership information) that are still under development/implementation, if possible, the institution should consider to use United States Postal Service (USPS) address standard format and USPS certified address validation services in U.S./Canada Post address standard format and address validation services in Canada

- The commercial data purchased from the third parties (such as HIDTA/HIFCA data) should be consistent or compatible with other institution's reference data

It is worth mentioning that financial institutions could take advantage of other industry or institution-wide initiatives such as Legal Entity Identification (LEI) (ISO 17442:2012) initiatives.

Legal entity identification is an integrated and necessary component of financial services transactions. Entering into business relationships requires KYC processes to be initiated and maintained for the duration of these relationships and any longer term data retention requirements to be addressed. Parties (or counter-parties) involved in financial transactions need to be identified within these transactions. In 2011, the Group of Twenty called on the Financial Stability Board (FSB) to provide recommendations for a global Legal Entity Identifier (LEI) and a supporting governance structure. This led to the development of the Global

LEI System (GLEIS) which, through the issuance of LEIs, now provides unique identification of legal entities participating in financial transactions across the globe. Each LEI is a 20-digit alphanumeric code and associated set of six reference data items to uniquely identify a legally distinct entity that engages in financial market activities. This global standard meets the 2012 specifications of the ISO 17442:2012.

By using a global LEI system, financial institutions could clearly identify entity type customers and their counterparties, gain operational efficiencies (e.g., reducing the volume of transaction failures; lowering data cleansing, aggregation and reconciliation costs; reducing reporting costs etc.) and improve internal risk management.

Data frequency and timeliness

Typically daily source data refresh in AML platforms is enough for AML compliance requirements, but for fraud and certain financial crime risk management situations, real-time or near real time data refresh is necessary.

Data reconciliation

Even though AML related data is mainly used for AML compliance (and/or financial crime risk management) purpose, to avoid the incomplete or inaccurate information, the institution should perform the AML data reconciliation with data in other systems (e.g., the AML related financial transaction data could reconcile with the general ledger (GL) or other finance systems).

With proper current/future state and gap analysis as well as sufficient data profiling to examine the AML compliance required data available in an existing data source (e.g., a database or a file) and collect statistics and information about that data, the key stakeholders in an AML information systems implementation could draft the business requirements.

BUSINESS REQUIREMENTS

When the key stakeholders in an AML information systems implementation write the business requirements document (BRD), they need to keep few

AML specific items in mind in addition to the common requirements management best practices:

- Unlike traditional BRD for homegrown software development, there are at least two components in the implementation that are very likely needed to be purchased from third party vendors, i.e., watch-list/adverse media screening software and transaction monitoring software. So some requirements in the BRD could be used in the Request for Proposal (RFP) process.

- Also due to the fact that certain software components and commercial data (such as watch-lists and adverse media data) are going to be purchased from third party vendors, the BRD may need to be modified and refined after the contracts are awarded to the selected vendors and vendors' requirements gathering workshops are completed.

- The source data Extract, Transform and Load (ETL) development for the implementation may be performed by an internal team or by a service provider; actually the latter is a common case if the financial institution's core systems (such as core banking systems/wire transaction systems) are maintained by external service providers. Therefore, the requirements management protocols and processes (including change controls) need to be clearly set up and specified in the BRD.

A typical BRD of an AML information systems implementation covers the following non-exhaustive topics:

- Purpose and Background

- Scope

  - In Scope

  - Out of Scope

- Assumptions

- Constraints

- Dependencies

- Implementation Risks

- Business/Compliance Benefits

- Business Analysis Approach

  ◦ Current State

  ◦ Future State

  ◦ Gaps and Bridges

- Business Requirements Sources and Business Requirements Traceability

- Detailed Business Requirements

  ◦ Functional Requirements

    ▪ Customer Screening Requirements

      - Name/Attribute Matching (Entity Resolution) Algorithms

      - Watch-list and Adverse Media Data

    ▪ Transaction Monitoring Requirements

      - Dynamic Risk Rating and Due Diligent

      - Unusual Activity Detection

      - Network Analysis

      - Peer Group Analysis

      - Alert and Case Management

- Other Financial Crime Risk Management Modules (such as FATCA, Fraud, if required)

  - Workflow Requirements

  - Record Management Requirements

  - Regulatory Reporting Requirements

  - Internal Reporting Requirements

  - Audit Trail Requirements

  - Source Data Requirements

  - Data ETL Processing Requirements

  - Data Conversion/Migration Requirements

- Other Requirements

  - Interface Requirements

  - Hardware/Software Requirements

  - Information Security Requirements

  - Performance Requirements

  - Recovery Requirements

  - Operational Requirements

- Business Requirements Management

- Related Documents

COTS and Vendor Selections

Many components in an AML information systems implementation are either COTS (commercial off-the-shelf) software or COTS data services. On the surface, it seems that a COTS implementation might be a very simple one – purchase the COTS packages and make them work in the financial institution's environment. However in reality, COTS implementation can be very risky and challenging.

COTS software is used to reduce development time, lower systems costs and gain continual product improvement in functionality and capability of the system. Typically, COTS software has the following characteristics:

- Developed and supplied by an external vendor or vendors

- Sold, leased or licensed to an acquiring organization

- Tailored to meet business requirements and used by the end business users in the acquiring organization

- Integrated into the IT infrastructure and architectures of the acquiring organization unless an application service provider (ASP) model or Software as a Service (SaaS) is used

- Supported and evolved by the vendor(s)

- Has a profit driven commercial product

- Its life cycle could be impacted by market pressures and economic conditions

A COTS software implementation may have many potential risks:

- The acquiring organization is not the developer or even the owner of the COTS software, thus has no control over the functionality, performance and evolution of the COTS product.

- Very often, either the business requirements need to be bent to fit the COTS software or significant effort is required to customize the COTS software to meet the business requirements.

- Sometimes, extra effort is required for the acquiring organization to build hardware infrastructure and/or develop software interfaces to incorporate COTS components.

- The acquiring organization has to track the vendor product releases, configuration management and ongoing training within the implementation duration and beyond.

To mitigate these risks, it is desired and essential to use a thorough procurement process such as Request for Proposal (RFP) to select a suitable vendor or vendors.

A typical RFP contains the following non-exhaustive sections:

- Project Overview and Administrative Information

- Functional and Technical Requirements

- Management Requirements

- Vendor Qualifications and References

- Vendor Section

- Pricing Section

- Contracts (or Master Service Agreements (MSAs)) and Licenses

There are many factors that key stakeholders of a financial institution need to consider when they start the RFP and vendor selection process for the AML information systems implementation:

- Not all COTS software packages are created equal, therefore performing a market scan of potential vendors is well worth the investment. Based on the current state, future state and gap analysis as well as the business requirements specified in BRD, the implementation team would know the business needs (including but not limited to compliance requirements, operational processes etc.), the existing IT architecture and technology capacity, the inventory of the source data systems, the quality, volume and the estimated growth rate of the available source data as well as potential pain points on both business and technology sides. Then the implementation team could scrutinize the vendor landscape in AML information systems domain. Many commercial market reports would be a good information source about AML systems vendors, such as references [54-61].

- In most cases a financial institution may not want state of the art COTS components; but mature ones that fit the institution's specific AML compliance needs. The vendor evaluation and selection criteria could and should be created for the RFP process. The rationale of the evaluation and selection is to determine:

    ◦ A vendor's products and services meet the institution's business requirements and compliance needs without heavy customization (typically over customization will not only cost more but also cause ongoing maintenance headaches)

    ◦ A vendor understands the requirements and implementation tasks against the institution's statement of work or use cases

    ◦ A vendor has the appropriate pricing models for required functionality (for example, the implementation team not only needs to consider the one-time project cost of the COTS software, but also the maintenance cost after the deployment)

    ◦ A vendor's technologies are compatible with the institution's existing or planned IT and/or data architecture and capacity

    ◦ A vendor has adequate and relevant experience in both compliance and technology areas for similar implementations

○ A vendor can demonstrate appropriate management/
implementation skills to meet deadlines with knowledgeable
resources

○ A vendor has an established industry presence, reasonable
market share, stable financial investment for ongoing research
and development (R & D)/innovation, good references/
reputations as well as the ability to adapt to changes in
regulatory requirements and money laundering typologies

○ A vendor can provide good ongoing support

An emerging trend is to evaluate vendors on the completeness and
responsiveness of their management plans and the team assigned to the
implementation. And special consideration should be given to vendors
who propose a detailed plan with sufficient breakdown of tasks and steps
to demonstrate a complete understanding of the implementation.

And there are many lessons that the key stakeholders of a financial
institution could learn from other institutions' implementations:

- There is a tendency for vendors to oversell. So in addition to
  the statement of work, the implementation team could provide
  vendors with end-to-end use cases/scenarios and request vendors
  to demonstrate the proposals/proof of concept (PoC) against the
  detailed use cases/scenarios.

- The implementation team should have a big picture – always keep
  enterprise wide requirements and life cycle issues in mind. For
  example, instead of finding a vendor's products or services that
  only cover a group or a divisional level narrow needs but ones that
  could be used by the whole enterprise.

- Flexibility with respect to requirements is vital for a COTS
  software implementation. COTS software packages may guide
  or even dictate the requirements to some extent. So learning from
  vendors about industry emerging trends in the RFP process is a

great opportunity, and then the requirements could be modified/refined accordingly.

- The implementation team should manage the trade-off between requirements and COTS software customization to avoid potential problems and realize the benefits of COTS software packages.

- Gaining vendor cooperation occurs before the contract is signed and the ongoing vendor relationship management is very important to the successful implementation of the COTS software.

The following are some (non-exhaustive) technical questions that the key stakeholders of a financial institution could think about or could ask potential vendors during the RFP process:

Software delivery model

- What is a vendor's software delivery model? On-premises? Or as a SaaS (or a cloud-based solution)? Or hybrid?

- If a vendor's software delivery model is SaaS or hybrid (i.e., with a SaaS component), then where and how is the data stored, accessed, processed and protected? Is the data center in a foreign jurisdiction? Did the data center or the vendor pass any service audit and/or security certification such as Statement on Auditing Standards No. 70 (SAS 70)/Statements on Standards for Attestation Engagements No. 16 (SSAE 16) audit and SysTrust/WebTrust certification? Will the institution share the hosting environment with other financial institutions? What are the detailed Service Level Agreements (SLAs) for the hosting services?

- If the software delivery model of a vendor is on premise, then what are the IT infrastructure (hardware, network, computer operation systems, storage devices, etc.) requirements? What would be 3-5 years capacity planning for the required IT infrastructure?

Model risk management evidence

- The U.S. OCC/FRB "Supervisory Guidance on Model Risk Management" directs that a vendor's products should be incorporated into a bank's broader model risk management framework, and "Banks should require the vendor to provide developmental evidence explaining the product components, design, and intended use, to determine whether the model is appropriate for the bank's products, exposures, and risks." So the implementation team should request a vendor's developmental evidence regarding its products/systems and ask "What are the systems (model) limitations?"

- Can a vendor's products be incorporated into the broader model risk management framework in other financial services areas (such as asset/investment management, securities trading and insurance) in addition to banking services within the institution?

Watch-list screening

- What are the name/attribute matching (i.e., entity resolution) algorithms supported by the watch-list screening software? Do those algorithms cover most of name/attribute variations (please see Appendix A. for technical details about name/attribute variations) based on the institution's ethnic diversity of the customer base and operational environment?

- Does a watch-list screening software vendor also provide watch-list data and/or adverse media data services? If not, which and how the third party commercial watch-list data and/or adverse media data sets does the screening software support?

- Does a watch-list screening software module allow the institution to have flexible configurations/matching rules (such as use additional attribute, use different matching algorithms for different incoming data sets, adjust matching scores per customer segmentation etc.) to reduce false positive alerts?

- Can a watch-list screening software module support a homegrown (either a black or a white) list?

- How does a watch-list screening software module automatically refresh watch-list data?

- How does a watch-list screening software module schedule automatic screening jobs?

- How does a watch-list screening software module perform adverse media screening?

- How does a watch-list screening software module integrate with a transaction monitoring software module from the same vendor or another vendor? For example, can the watch-list screening software perform the real-time transaction related watch-list screening?

- What are the performance benchmark results of a watch-list screening software module against a certain size data set (e.g., against a data set which has a volume similar to the institution's customer data set)?

- Does the watch-list screening software provide a detailed audit trail?

Transaction monitoring

- Does a transaction monitoring software module have a built-in library of detection scenarios that covers the institution's compliance needs and common AML red flags? Are those "standard" detection scenarios modifiable? Are new detection scenarios allowed to be created in the system?

- Can a transaction monitoring software module detect the large currency transactions (with the feature to exempt customers) automatically?

- Can a transaction monitoring software module detect the large currency transactions for foreign currencies and/or foreign customers?

- Can a transaction monitoring software module detect the large currency transactions by aggregating all currency transactions (e.g., debit card, ATM, cash in foreign currencies etc.)?

- Does a transaction monitoring software module support dynamic risk rating and risk-based due diligence? If yes, then how does it work?

- Does a transaction monitoring software module support the network analysis? If yes, then to what extent and how?

- Does a transaction monitoring software module support the peer group analysis? If yes, then how does it work?

- Does a transaction monitoring software module support other financial services areas (such as asset/investment management, securities trading and insurance) in addition to banking services within the institution?

- Does a transaction monitoring software module support the detection of other financial crimes (such as fraud, market abuse etc.) in addition to AML scenarios?

- Can a transaction monitoring software module efficiently monitor real-time or near real-time transactions?

- What are the performance benchmark results of a transaction monitoring module against various data sets?

- Does a transaction monitoring software module provide a detailed audit trail?

Workflow, alert and case management

- What workflows does a case management software module support?

- Can a case management software module handle both watch-list screening alerts and transaction monitoring alerts?

- Can a case management software module perform automatic prioritization and/or routing of alerts based on certain rules?

- Is there a mechanism to rank the importance of alerts and order the sequence of investigations in a case management software module?

- Does a case management software module allow the institution to set up flexible configurations to support existing business/compliance processes without programming level customization?

- What type of actions can be taken to perform investigations for alerts/cases in a case management software module?

- What supporting information can be stored and/or linked in a case management software module?

- Can the alerts/cases information be linked to other alerts/cases or even be exported to external systems in a case management software module?

- Does a case management software module provide a detailed audit trail? What actions are tracked for audit purposes? How to archive and retrieve relevant investigation records that allow quick and easy responses to regulating agencies, auditors and other interested parties?

- How does a case management software module allow compliance team members to work collaboratively under the principles of segregation of duties?

Regulatory and management reports

- Which jurisdiction (U.S., Canada, etc.) does a reporting software module support? And what regulatory reports does it support for the corresponding jurisdiction?

- Does a reporting software module support automated data populating, data/information validation, report filing/refiling (in single or batch mode submission) and acknowledgement recording for regulatory reports (such as CTR/LCTR and SAR/STR)?

- Does a reporting software module support a secure connection to regulator's (such as FinCEN's or FINTRAC's) reporting tools or websites?

- Does a reporting software module support historical CTR/LCTR fillings?

- Can a reporting software module be integrated with workflow and alert/case management module?

- Does a reporting software module provide a detailed audit trail for reporting activity?

- Does a reporting software module provide a dashboard for AML compliance summary information?

- What built-in management/productivity reports does a reporting software module provide?

- How to modify the built-in management/productivity reports and how to create ad hoc/new management/productivity reports in the reporting software module?

Security and permissions

- Does a vendor's AML software support the Single Sign-On (SSO) by using the enterprise security (such as Network ID/LDAP integration)?

- Does a vendor's AML software support role based user/permission management?

- What is the overall security mechanism/model to protect data and sensitive information in a vendor's AML software?

Systems integration and user experience

- What administrative features does a vendor's AML software provide?

- Which input data format does a vendor's AML software support for data ingestion? And what are the input data requirements for the implementation?

- What data elements/information could be exported from a vendor's AML software and in which format(s)?

- Are there any systems interfaces (such as web services, APIs) to external systems from a vendor's AML software? If yes, then how to use them?

- Are the user interfaces (UIs) of a vendor's AML software intuitive and easy to navigate?

- Does a vendor's AML software support the personalization of user interfaces without any customization at programming/code level?

- Does a vendor's AML software support user friendly search functionality for certain information (e.g., customer, account, transaction etc.)?

Ongoing operations

- What are the operational tasks/scheduled jobs for a vendor's AML software?

- What is the suggested data backup/restore approach from an AML software vendor?

- What are the suggested Business Continuity/Disaster Recovery plans from an AML software vendor? Are the plans adequate to avoid unacceptable disruptions?

Training and documentation

- Does an AML software vendor provide any training to the implementation team, IT support group and end business users?

- What are the vendor's training topics and when will the training be provided? Who is the audience of the training?

- Does a vendor provide all the necessary AML software documentation (including but not limited to product specifications, configuration management etc.)?

Patches, upgrades and ongoing support

- What is the product roadmap of a vendor's AML software?

- How often does an AML software vendor release a minor or major version patch and/or upgrade?

- How should a patch and/or an upgrade be implemented?

- How does an AML software vendor provide ongoing support? What are the SLAs?

SYSTEMS SPECIFICATIONS, ARCHITECTURE AND DESIGN

After AML software vendors and/or data service providers are selected and contracts are awarded, the implementation team could refine and finalize the business requirements by taking extra considerations of features/products/services provided by vendors. Also vendors usually would hold some workshop sessions on-site to gather baseline/interface requirements for the implementation of components that they are responsible for.

And then internal IT groups and/or vendors' delivery teams need to draft System Requirements Specifications (SRS, AKA Software Requirements Specifications) for all major components of the implementation. A non-exhaustive is as follows:

- SRS of IT infrastructure

- SRS of source data ETL processes (including but not limited to, data dictionary, data mapping, ETL stages and controls etc.)

- SRS of watch-list screening module

- SRS of transaction monitoring module

- SRS of workflow and alert/case management module

- SRS of regulatory and management reporting module

- SRS of other system modules (such as system access controls, database backup and restore, scheduled batch jobs, system logs and audit trails, etc.)

In order to assure the to-be-implemented AML information systems work as expected per business/compliance requirements, it is crucial to map all required data elements properly and correctly. This requires the implementation team members have a solid understanding about available data in source systems (such as a core banking system) and input data requirements in target AML systems (such as a transaction monitoring system). For example, all required transaction codes in core banking systems need to be correctly mapped to acceptable transaction codes in a transaction monitoring system so that all transaction related scenario detections could work properly.

After system specifications are embodied, the implementation team (more specifically, the institution's internal IT groups and/or vendors' delivery teams) need to define the conceptual system architecture and carry out detailed system design.

The technical nature of AML information systems is data mining and electronic discovery (eDiscovery), which, strictly speaking, is different from the Business Intelligence (BI) applications for finance or marketing although they may share some common data elements and data management processes. There are many industry methodologies and frameworks in data mining and eDiscovery areas, such as Cross Industry Standard Process for Data Mining (CRISP-DM) and Electronic Discovery Reference Model (EDRM). Instead of describing the industry general approaches to data mining and discovery related system architecture and design, in the rest of this subsection, two concrete examples are given to demonstrate the system architecture and design considerations during the implementation of AML information systems.

A single customer view

Some financial institutions may already have a holistic view of all customers across all LOBs, and the single view of all customers is critical for AML compliance (e.g., to monitor all aggregated transactions across multiple LOBs for a given customer). But some financial institutions may not have a consolidated data hub to provide a single view of all customers for various reasons (e. g., due to the cost and technical complexity of data consolidation, or even regulatory restrictions between different sectors such as banking and insurance). If regulations permit, then how can the implementation team create a single view of all customers across all LOBs?

Let's take individual type customers as an example to depict the corresponding architecture and design considerations of customer information consolidation (AKA consolidated Customer Information File (CIF) in the banking industry):

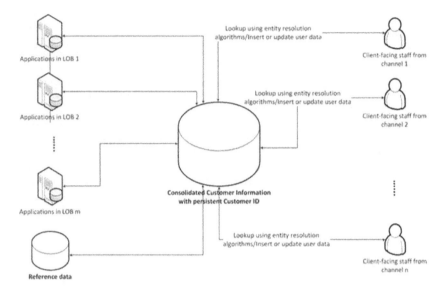

Figure-5-1 A Single View of Individual Customers

With the single view of all customers across all LOBs, when a customer is on board to open a new account or obtain a new service, frontline personnel need to look up the customer using name/attributes (such as address, SSN/SIN/TIN, DoB etc.) in a consolidated customer information database (if such a database does not exist across the LOBs, then the institution could use the most widely used or the most reliable Customer Relationship Management (CRM) database within the institution as the initial baseline database). If a matched customer record is found in the consolidated customer information database, then this customer is an existing one and his/her information needs to be appended or updated accordingly; otherwise, this customer is a brand new customer and the new customer record with all necessary information needs to be created in the consolidated customer information database. When an existing customer wants to make any changes (e.g., close an account) for his/her accounts or services, frontline personnel in the institution also need to look up the customer using name/attributes in the consolidated customer information database and make the updates accordingly.

The above-mentioned architecture and design considerations for individual type customers' data consolidation seem simple, but in reality, it is non-trivial or difficult to find proper matching rules/algorithms. Moreover, things get pretty complicated if customer data needs to be consolidated for households (i.e., to perform the process of grouping customers to form certain decision units) and/or entity type customers where hierarchical relationships may need to be introduced.

Data feeds directly from sources or from data hubs

Some financial institutions may already have a data hub or hubs (e.g., a data warehouse or data marts) as the required information source for the implementation. But some financial institutions may not have a data hub or data hubs as the upstream data sources for the implementation, in this situation, should the implementation team build an intermediate data hub for the feeds to the AML information systems?

There are tradeoffs in making the decision based on the numbers and complexities of upstream and downstream systems/applications:

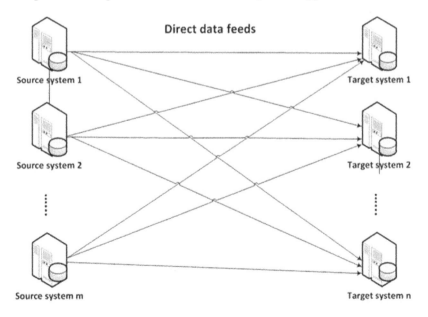

Figure-5-2 Direct Feeds

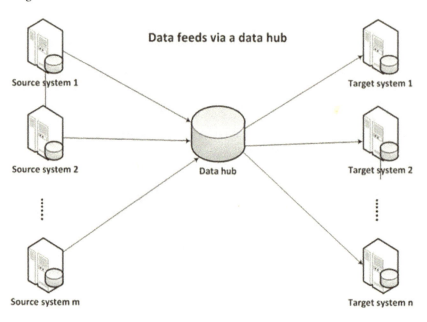

Figure-5-3 Feeds via a Data Hub

	Pros	**Cons**
Direct feeds	• Only the (exact) target system required data sets need be extracted so the file sizes are smaller and time to market is quicker	• If there are many upstream (source) systems and many downstream (target) systems, then the processes of direct feeds could be difficult, more expensive and less efficient to manage and maintain

| Data feeds from a hub | • Common data elements in the hub could be shared by multiple target systems

• More data management features could be built in the hub (such as delta extracting logic, data reconciliation etc.)

• Overall ongoing maintenance cost could be lower

• It is relatively flexible to adapt changes (e.g., sometimes the changes are only required in the hub, not in source systems) | • The initial development cost and time for building the hub could be higher and longer since all relevant data (may contain information not used for AML systems) in all source (upstream) systems needs to be identified, mapped, extracted, transformed and loaded into the hub for shared services |

Table-5-2 Direct Data Feeds vs. Data Feeds via a Hub

So for a small bank with very limited source systems (e.g., only two upstream systems – core banking and wire transfer systems) and very limited target systems (e.g., only one AML information system), the direct feeds approach is a cost effective solution. While for a big bank (such as an international bank), the approach of using a data hub or data hubs for shared services (to AML, fraud, market abuse, operational risk etc.) makes perfect sense.

It is worth mentioning that there are many architecture and design considerations actually depend on the features of vendors' products or services. For example, for the ongoing source data extracts, should the files be full data extracts or just delta data extracts (i.e., only the records that have changes – new or updated or "deleted" ones are in the files)? If a vendor's products/services do not have delta detection logic or feature, then delta extracts may have to be created for the implementation. The implementation team should handle those types of questions on a case by case basis.

SYSTEMS BUILDING

For an implementation of AML information systems, typically, various parties are responsible for the development of their respective components:

- IT infrastructure groups need to build the necessary infrastructure for different environments (development, testing and production etc.) per the specifications, system architecture and design if the software delivery model is not SaaS

- Vendors need to perform configuration tasks or even make programming level changes per the specifications, system architecture and design for required out-of-box features or certain customizations in watch-list screening and transaction monitoring modules

- The team members (of internal IT resources and/or external service providers) need to build the end-to-end ETL processes to generate necessary data sets for the implementation

In the rest of this subsection, instead of zooming into vendor-dependent or particular system-dependent development topics, the model development (an integral part of system building) is elaborated as the continuation of technical discussions started in "AML Typologies and Models" subsection.

Typically the initial threshold values/scores of the detection scenarios' parameters are specified in the BRD and/or SRS documents, and those initial numbers are possibly coming from:

- Regulatory requirements (such as $10,000 for CTR/LCTR reporting)

- Institution's past experience (such as SAR/STR fillings etc.) or even from existing screen/monitoring systems if the implementation is in the nature of enhancements or migration for existing AML information systems

- Suggestions given by vendors

- Knowledge shared by published industry research and/or peer financial institutions

- Initial data analysis for the implementation (such as basic data distribution statistics of customers, accounts, transactions and expected activities etc.)

During the system building stage (or model development stage), the implementation team could adjust certain initial threshold values/scores of the detection scenarios with the availability of enough representative data. Two detailed examples are given below.

Watch-list screening scores

Good watch-list screening software usually uses a parameter/indicator "confidence level score" to measure how closely the interested entity information matches an entity's information on a watch-list. And the confidence level score is not necessary a percentage, but for convenience, most watch-list screening software vendors often use "confidence level score = 100" to indicate an exact match. The confidence level scores may vary with many factors, such as:

- Entity resolution algorithms available in the software packages

- Detailed matching rules (which usually are specified in BRD and/ or SRS documents)

- Data available for the matching process (i.e., entity data within the watch-lists and entity data available in the institution)

The required data available in the institution and/or watch-lists may only have partial identifying information in addition to names – such as addresses, identification numbers, gender, and age. So even though a confidence level score or confidence level scores were pre-specified in requirements documents, in the system building stage, the implementation team could try different combinations of algorithms, attributes (e.g., names plus addresses plus gender plus DoB) and rules (e.g., names matched and DoB within +/- one year etc.) to derive the proper confidence level score(s) for when a matching alert should be generated. Of course, if better confidence level scores are derived, then the implementation team should document the changes as well as the rationales in the corresponding sections of BRD and/or SRS documents.

Above-the-Line (ATL) and Below-the-Line (BTL) analysis

If it wasn't fully done to evaluate the efficacy of calculated thresholds for certain detection scenarios during the initial analysis stage, then the implementation team could perform the Above-the-Line (ATL) and Below-the-Line (BTL) analysis (also called ATL/BTL testing) in the system building stage with the availability of enough representative data.

Above/Below the line analysis is the process of testing of an AML model (such as a detection scenario) just above/below the pre-selected threshold value(s). Basically it is used to determine whether the threshold can be raised/reduced (usually by multiples of standard deviation) and alerts of 'suspicious' activities are not missed after the threshold adjustment. For example, if in a detection scenario, the "aggregated amount of ATM transactions higher than $5,000" is specified in BRD and/or SRS document, then the implementation team could perform an ATL assessment for any statistically significant changes of 'suspicious' activity alerts if the threshold is set to $6,000 or $7,000 or so on against enough available data. Again, if the better threshold values are found via ATL/BTL analysis, then the implementation team should document the changes as well as the rationales in the corresponding sections of BRD and/or SRS documents.

SYSTEMS TESTING

The testing process allows the institution to affirm that the to-be implemented AML information systems will not only perform as specified, but also satisfy the institution's business/compliance requirements and operate successfully within the overall information systems and data processing environment.

There are many available software testing/QA methodologies and frameworks. In this subsection, the modified V-model (which includes operations and maintenance part) is discussed.

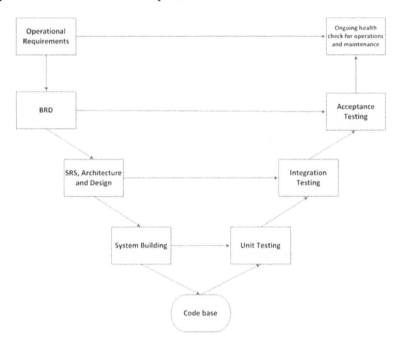

Figure-5-4 Modified V-Model

For an implementation of AML information systems, typically, the parties who are responsible for the development of their respective components should perform the unit testing for their own components.

The to-be-implemented AML information systems are usually subject to System Integration Testing (SIT) and User Acceptance Testing (UAT, AKA Business Acceptance Test (BAT) or Client Acceptance Test (CAT)) before the systems are approved for use.

SIT testing is conducted on an integrated or complete AML information system to verify and validate its conformance to technical specifications, architecture and design documents.

UAT testing is performed by business users to validate the complete AML information systems with sufficient history data meet business requirements via QA tasks such as security access testing, functionality testing, data validation, and an appropriate level regression testing if parameters/configurations have changed after the system tuning based on the initial history data.

In a Systems Development Life Cycle or Software Development Life Cycle (SDLC), entry and exit criteria are the set of conditions that should be met in order to commence and close a testing/QA phase or stage.

Typical SIT entry criteria are:

- All knowledge transfer activities, if any, have been completed

- All SIT test cases/test scripts and expected results for SIT have been prepared and documented

- Unit testing is completed and all critical defects found during Unit testing have been fixed and verified

- All test data sets are prepared and ready to be imported

- SIT environment is fully functional and accessible

- Code, configuration/ interface(s)/required batch jobs have been promoted to SIT and are stable

- All SIT testing and supporting resources are acquired

- Procedures for test/defect management and escalation are documented, reviewed and agreed by the implementation team

Typical SIT exit criteria are:

- All intended test cases/test scripts have been executed as per the test plan(s)

- All test results have been documented for review and/or approval

- All test defects have been documented and all fixes have been re-tested and confirmed

- All outstanding high severity defects have been fixed and closed or there is an agreement with the business to fix them during the UAT

- Lessons learned have been documented/reviewed and improvements/corrective actions have been taken, as appropriate

Typical UAT entry criteria are:

- All test cases/test scripts (including Regression Testing if necessary) have been executed completely in SIT

- All high severity outstanding defects that are detected during SIT have been fixed and closed or there is an agreement with the business to fix them during the UAT

- UAT testing environment set up (including the importing of the test data) is completed and operational

- The Test Plan and associated documents have been accepted by the business/compliance

- All UAT test cases/test scripts and expected results are documented and reviewed prior to the UAT

- All UAT testing and supporting resources are acquired

- UAT (business/compliance) testers have been given system access instructions, UAT test schedule and test cases/test scripts

Typical UAT exit criteria are:

- All the intended test cases/test scripts regarding configurations/code units/interfaces/required batch jobs have been executed

- All fixes for given configurations/code units/interfaces/required jobs have been tested/re-tested and confirmed

- All outstanding high severity defects of that are detected during UAT have been fixed and closed or there is an agreement with the business to fix them at a future date

- Lessons learned have been documented/reviewed and improvements/corrective actions have been taken, as appropriate

- Testing results are signed off by appropriate stakeholders

For an AML information system or AML information systems, the SIT and UAT should focus on correctness (ability to process information according to prescribed requirements and rules), completeness (such as data completeness), security (against accidental and/or intentional modifications or misuse), usability and auditability. For example, the testing could cover the following non-exhaustive areas:

- System access

- Configuration settings

- Reference data (including but not limited to watch-lists and adverse media data)

- Data extracts

- Watch-list and adverse media screening

- Transaction monitoring detection scenarios

- Workflow and alert/case management

- Regulatory and management information reporting

- Logs and audit trails

- Scheduled (batch) jobs and ongoing maintenance services

Two concrete testing/QA examples are given below.

Accuracy testing of watch-list screening

Technically speaking, the watch-list and adverse media screening is about entity resolution in nature. So the implementation team and/or business users could use a sample entity data set that contains some known records on watch-lists (say, on a PEP list) with some name/attribute variations listed in Appendix A. to test the accuracy of various search results. Either a simple matching rate in terms of percentage or the metrics listed in Appendix A. (such as Precision, Recall, etc.) could be used to measure the accuracy of testing results.

Data ETL processes check

Ideally, if possible, the implementation team should build independent database query scripts to test the data in authoritative sources was extracted correctly per the business requirements, data mapping and input data requirements in the ETL processes. But if this is not technically feasible for whatever reasons, then the implementation team should at least use the expected data volume (e.g., various record counts) and representative sample data sets from authoritative sources to make sure the sample data flows from the authoritative sources to the AML information systems correctly as expected.

Deployment

After the successful completion of the SIT/UAT and with required approvals by key stakeholders, the implementation team could deploy all the system components (the third parties' modules, ETL packages, all required data, etc.) into the production environment.

DATA LOADING OR MIGRATION

For an implementation of AML information systems, certain current and history data (e.g., transaction data for previous many months) is required. In most cases the required data is loaded periodically (daily, weekly, etc.) into the systems using input files, but for certain cases the real-time or near real-time data fetching and loading is necessary (e.g., for monitoring near real-time wire transfers). And the initial loading of all necessary external data (such as external reference data, watch-lists, etc.) and internal data (about customers, accounts, transactions, etc.) could be time consuming due to the high volume of incoming data. And on an ongoing basis, full data extracts and/or delta extracts need to be loaded into the AML information systems for continuous AML compliance.

If the implementation is about the enhancements or migration of existing AML information systems, then the conversion and/or migration the corresponding data to the new environment might be required.

During the deployment stage, in addition to the initial loading of one time baseline data, the implementation team should perform all necessary tasks to deploy all required scheduled/automated (batch) jobs to assure the successful loading of data feeds going forward.

With all system components and required data in place within the production environment, the enriched AML compliance related data (such as behavior/statistical profiles, alerts etc.) and system related data (such as database index files, system logs etc.) would be generated continuously.

CONFIGURATION SETTINGS

Configuration management is critical for COTS components since all configuration settings are designed, developed, tested and initially tuned for fitting the particular business/compliance needs of the institution. The implementation team not only needs to deploy the approved configuration settings into the production environment properly and correctly but also needs to document deployed configuration settings sufficiently and share the configuration documents with respective vendors. This will ensure the vendors have the same configuration settings to rebuild a similar environment on vendors' side for ongoing support purposes (e.g., debugging for any defects in vendors' own environments).

PRODUCTION READINESS CHECK

After the production environment of AML information systems is ready (i.e., the necessary IT infrastructure, all required data, all scheduled batch jobs, exception handling modules etc. are deployed), the key stakeholders of the implementation need to perform the Post-Implementation Verification/ Validation (PIV) and operational readiness check.

The PIV is to ensure the soundness and readiness of the technology/data aspects of the production environment by verifying/validating it before it goes live, while the operational readiness check is about the people and process readiness for AML compliance operations after the deployment of AML information systems.

Before the production implementation goes live, all AML policies and procedures (especially those system related ones) need to be updated, distributed and communicated to all relevant parties within the institution.

Typically, right after the production implementation goes live, it is expected that one-time high volume alerts could be generated in the AML information systems. For example, the "white"/"good guys" lists for watch-list and adverse media screening need to be gradually built after the implementation. So enough well-trained compliance and supporting human resources need to be ready for the roll out of AML information systems implementation. Some financial institutions use a pilot implementation to learn about the AML information systems and enhanced compliance processes as well as to make necessary changes prior to full-scale implementation. But in any cases, AML compliance programs would need to process the alerts generated by the newly implemented AML information systems in a timely manner to meet compliance obligations.

INFORMATION SECURITY AND DATA PROTECTION

AML information systems contain not only the personally identifiable information (PII) but also the other regulated data (such as SAR/STR reports). Therefore the best practices of information security (InfoSec) risk management should be followed in the whole life cycle of the implementation, for example, the right sizing sample data should be depersonalized and masked before it is sent to the third party vendors for any testing purposes even though the vendors have already signed the non-disclosure agreements (NDAs).

Different financial institutions adopt different information security risk management standards, guidelines, policies and procedures (which are all related to InfoSec Confidentiality, Integrity and Availability (CIA) triad benchmark model). The institution and the implementation team should comply with all appropriate laws (such as Privacy Acts in different jurisdictions), regulations, internal policies and procedures in all environments, especially the production environment of AML information systems which contains the extremely sensitive AML and financial crime data.

BUSINESS CONTINUITY PLAN AND DISASTER RECOVERY PLAN

Regulators in both U.S. and Canada have time-sensitive AML regulatory reporting requirements. And if a real-time or near real-time monitoring module is enabled in the AML information systems, then an even higher availability of the systems is required.

Disaster recovery (DR) refers to specific steps taken to resume operations in the aftermath of a catastrophic natural disaster or national emergency while business continuity (BC) refers to an institution's ability to recover from an unexpected event and resume essential operations. And the industry trend is to combine the business-focused business continuity planning and technology-/infrastructure-focused disaster recovery planning into one.

The financial institution and implementation team need to assess the criticality and availability requirements of AML information systems based the institution's unique characteristics and compliance requirements and then put a business continuity plan (BCP) and disaster recovery plan(s) (DRP) in place.

Before the AML production systems implementation goes live, it is a best practice that not only the BCP/DRP documents (and all related policies and procedures) should be in place but also the BC/DR environment of AML information systems should be built and fully tested.

DOCUMENTATION AND TRAINING

Comprehensive documentation should be developed, updated and retained during and after the implementation of AML information systems per regulatory requirements as well as institution internal policies, procedures and processes. A non-exhaustive list of implementation related documents is as follows:

- Opportunity assessment/feasibility analysis (including but not limited to current state, future state and gap analysis)

- Project charter

- Detailed project and implementation plans (with scope, time, cost, quality, HR, risk, procurement (including but not limited to RFP and vendor management), communication and etc.)

- Business requirements document (BRD) and/or Statement of Work (SOW) document

- Specifications (including but not limited to the data requirements, data mapping with data lineage information, ETL related specifications, functional requirements of watch-list screening and transaction monitoring, non-functional requirements, such as file retention schedule, usability and etc.)

- IT and data architecture/solution overview (such as infrastructure layout, overall data flow, ETL architecture, vendors' model risk management evidence and etc.)

- Design documents (against the specifications of all major components in the implementation)

- Test/QA plan (including test cases and test scripts and all testing related items)

- System information security risk assessment and systems access process (including but not limited to information security controls) document

- Business/system workflow and typical use cases (including but not limited to use cases about internal controls and procedures)

- Change management documents (e.g., implementation change logs, enhancement related documents)

- Deployment planning and package deployment documents (including but not limited to deployment checklist, configuration steps, verification process and etc.)

- New or updated AML governance, policy and procedure documents

- All AML model risk management documents

- Training/handover/knowledge transfer materials and related documents (such as user manuals)

- Service Level Agreements (SLAs)/Operational Level Agreements (OLAs) with all external vendors and internal service providers

- Business Continuity Plan (BCP) and Disaster Recovery Plan (DRP)

- Maintenance planning documents (including but not limited to the ongoing scheduled batch jobs, and other maintenance items)

- Capacity planning documents (including but not limited to network storage, server CPU and memory capacity and etc.)

- Vendor's ongoing support contact info/support ticket system and procedures

- Internal ongoing support contact info/issue resolution procedures

- System change logs after the implementations

- Other project and implementation documents (such as contract agreements/MSAs, Non-Disclosure Agreements (NDAs), vendors' invoices, project audit results etc.)

As a pillar of a sound AML compliance program, the general AML training for appropriate personnel or all employees in the institution is critical. In terms of the AML information systems implementation, tailored training modules and materials at the necessary level should be provided to all key stakeholders of the implementation:

- General AML compliance training (regulatory requirements as well as institution internal policies, procedures and processes along with corresponding/supporting features in newly implemented AML information systems) to the operations personnel and other appropriate personnel

- Advanced AML compliance and investigation related training (regulatory requirements as well as institution internal policies, procedures and processes incorporated with corresponding/ supporting features in newly implemented AML information systems) to AML compliance team members

- Business/compliance administration related training (along with corresponding/supporting features in newly implemented AML information systems) to AML compliance program administrators

- Systems administration related technical training (incorporated with corresponding/supporting features/tasks in newly implemented AML information systems) to systems/database administrators

- General systems training (incorporated with corresponding/ supporting features in newly implemented AML information systems) to end business users of AML information systems, IT support team members, auditors/inspectors and other interested parties

Other learning opportunities could be explored and encouraged (such as knowledge transfer from vendor's consultants to internal support team members, peer Q & A sessions etc.) beyond the formal staff training.

Life After Production Deployment

With the successful production deployment of the AML information systems, financial institutions could realize many benefits for the AML compliance. By taking advantage of the AML information systems, AML compliance programs could build and/or enhance sustainable anti-money laundering operations through continuously operational optimization.

Support and Operations

Based on master service agreements (MSAs) between a financial institution and its AML information systems vendors/service providers, typically the vendors/service providers would fix any defects during a warranty period and continuously provide ongoing support within the contract terms. The institution's internal support groups would normally perform the system maintenance and operations per the operational level agreements (OLAs). For example, the internal IT infrastructure/data teams need to make sure all IT infrastructures (servers, network etc.) are in healthy conditions and every day's data ingestion, database indexing, AML behavior/statistical profiling are all successfully done per OLAs.

The IT infrastructure/data teams should try to automate routine system maintenance tasks (such as database backups) and operational tasks (such as input files archiving, auto-runs of scheduled batch jobs, automated notifications of system exceptions/errors etc.).

And the AML compliance team and internal support groups should work together to have sustainable AML compliance operations in place using AML information systems to avoid any compliance gaps/regulatory remediation. For instance, in addition to the interactive (real-time manual) name search against watch-lists and adverse media data during the customer onboarding process, the teams in the institution's various functions should work collaboratively to build operational (preferably automated) batch jobs to fetch all the required entity data (including but not limited to all regulatory specified parties, such as customers, Third-Party Service Providers (TPSPs), etc.) pertaining to the institution and all required watch-lists and adverse media data either on demand (e.g., whenever a notification of data changes is received) or periodically (e.g., weekly) and then to perform watch-list and adverse media screening per the following logic:

- If all required entity data pertaining to the institution is defined as the "source data set" and all required watch-lists and adverse media data is defined as the "target data set", then (1) whenever there is any change in "source data set" but no change in "target data set", then the changing part data in "source data set" (or the whole "source data set") should be scanned against the latest whole "target data set"; (2) whenever there is any change in "target data set" but no change in "source data set", then the latest whole "source data set" should be scanned against the changing part data in "target data set" (or the whole "target data set"); (3) whenever there is any change in "source data set" as well as there is any change in "target data set" at the same time, then the latest whole "source data set" should be scanned against the latest whole "target data set".

PERFORMANCE REPORTING AND BENCHMARKING

Just like some performance metrics (such as mean time to resolve by severity, downtime percentage, average number of affected users by incident severity etc.) could be used to determine the performance of IT services, the AML compliance program in a financial institution could and should use some key performance metrics to determine/benchmark the program's effectiveness and efficiency using the evidence in the AML information systems. Some common but non-exhaustive performance metrics are as follows:

- Case-to-Alert ratio[21] (by detection scenario/rule) = (Number of Cases)/(Number of Alerts): this indicator may reveal the quality of alerts (e.g., the high/low volume of false positive alerts)

- (Regulatory Report)-to-Case (such as SAR/STR-to-Case) ratio[21] (by case type) = (Number of Regulatory Reports)/(Number of Cases): this indicator may reveal the quality of cases (e.g., the high/low volume of reportable suspicious cases)

- (Regulatory Report)-to-(Other Sourced Case) ratio[21] (by case type) = (Number of Regulatory Reports)/(Number of Other Sourced Cases): this indicator may reveal the quality of other sourced cases (e.g., subpoenas, and law enforcement requests)

- Alerts generated by time period

- Cases generated by time period

- CTRs/LCTRs filed by time period

- SARs/STRs filed by time period

- Alerts/cases/regulatory reports generated by high risk customers (by time period)

---

[21] The types and subtypes of alerts/cases/reports should be applied consistently in order to make those metrics meaningful.

- Alerts/cases/regulatory reports generated by high risk geographic locations (by time period)

- Alerts/cases/regulatory reports generated by high risk delivery channels or products/services (by time period)

- Alerts/cases/regulatory reports generated by LOBs (by time period)

- Backlogs of alerts/cases/regulatory reports by time period

- Alerts/cases/reports completed/closed by person (by time period)

- Pending alerts/cases/reports by person (by time period)

- Overdue alerts/cases/reports by person (by time period)

With various standard benchmarks and certain quality management methodologies/frameworks (such as six sigma/lean process) in place, the AML compliance program with integrated people, process, technology and information (data) functions (and/or possibly with other anti-financial crime functions within the institution) could maximize the effectiveness and efficiency of ongoing AML compliance efforts against industry best practices and the institution's risk tolerance.

CALIBRATION AND ENHANCEMENTS

Even though AML information systems might already be initially tuned during the implementation stage, but the regular ongoing (e.g., every six months or one year, or whenever a significant change occurs) calibration and/or enhancements of those systems are necessary[22] to avoid inadvertent noncompliance due to constant regulatory, organizational and/or data changes such as:

---

[22] In U.S., the ongoing AML model validation process has received increasing attention from regulators. But the broad discussions of AML model risk management are beyond the scope of this book.

- New regulatory requirements have been introduced

- Significant regulatory examination or audit findings have been noted for the AML compliance program

- Customer base has been changed due to mergers and acquisitions (M & A)

- New delivery channels and/or products/services have been introduced

- The institution has expanded into new geographic areas

- New service providers have been used

- Compliance/operational processes have been updated/enhanced

- IT infrastructure/application/data services have been changed (e.g., changes occurred in upstream source systems)

- Major version upgrades of third party AML information systems have been deployed (with certain key changes in some modules)

The regular ongoing calibration and/or enhancements of AML information systems should also follow the best practices discussed in this chapter and all previous chapters. Again the ultimate goal is to meet AML regulatory compliance in the most effective and efficient way with evidence: catch the bad guys and reportable suspicious/unusual activities as well as reduce the false positive alarms.

For example, special attentions could be given to the following situations:

- Compliance gaps (e.g., gaps of detection scenarios) due to the introduction of new regulatory requirements

- Deficiencies in alerts/cases/SARs or STRs identified by examiners/inspectors or internal/external auditors

- No or very few alerts have been generated for high risk customers after a particular point in time (i.e., dynamic risk rating and risk based due diligence is no longer optimized)

- Customer behavior patterns and trends have been changed due to the changes of the customer base

- A detection scenario no longer triggers any new alerts after a particular point in time

- A particular product/service or transaction code has no alerts after a particular point in time

- A high (or higher) percentage of recurring or similar alerts that were previously investigated and deemed not suspicious/unusual after a particular point in time

- Vendors' development evidence of model risk management has been changed for their key features in their upgraded modules

The internal resources in the AML compliance program and support groups along with the necessary external resources could perform the following analysis, testing, tuning and possible enhancements:

- Add the necessary (fully tested) new detection scenarios to cover the regulatory gaps or identified deficiencies

- Remove those detection scenarios that no longer fit the regulatory requirements or no longer valid for the compliance program

- Identify the common patterns in false positive alerts/low quality cases and make necessary adjustments

- Identify the common patterns in confirmed suspicions/unusual activities and extend the coverage for the patterns to all relevant detection scenarios

- Perform the sensitivity analysis (i.e., to check the impact on the outputs of an AML model that can be apportioned to different changes in its inputs) for certain parameters/thresholds of detection scenarios and make necessary adjustments for those parameters/thresholds

- Perform the segmentation analysis for the new/changed customer base and re-optimize dynamic risk rating and risk based due diligence

- Identify the new characteristics of peer groups for the new/changed customer base and make appropriate adjustments for existing peer groups

- Combine the ATL/BTL analysis and other data analysis methods against certain detection scenarios (e.g., not only raise/reduce the thresholds but also add/remove filters for non-performing or poorly performing detection scenarios) and make appropriate adjustments

- Perform a thorough data profiling and impact analysis if source data has significant changes, and make all necessary changes to the watch-list screening rules and transaction monitoring detection scenarios

All the ongoing calibration and/or enhancements of AML information systems should be well-documented, all relevant personnel should be trained with the changes and enhancements, and all relevant parties should be communicated per the institution's compliance governance model, policies and procedures.

An addendum: This book was a work between late 2015 and early 2016. As we all know, regulatory compliance is an ever changing space. Right before this book was submitted to the printer for printing, the customer due diligence (CDD) final rules were released in the U.S. on May 6, 2016.

The U.S. Treasury Department's FinCEN released CDD final rules under the Bank Secrecy Act (BSA) to clarify and strengthen customer due diligence requirements for: banks; brokers or dealers in securities; mutual funds; and futures commission merchants and introducing brokers in commodities. The rules contain explicit customer due diligence requirements and include a new requirement to identify and verify the identity of beneficial owners of legal entity customers, subject to certain exclusions and exemptions. And the "covered financial institutions" must comply with these rules by May 11, 2018. Therefore, "the FinCEN new beneficial ownership rule" discussed in Chapter 5 has become "the to-be-implemented beneficial ownership rule" in U.S.: Specifically, the rule contains three core requirements: (1) identifying and verifying the identity of the beneficial owners of companies opening accounts; (2) understanding the nature and purpose of customer relationships to develop customer risk profiles; and (3) conducting ongoing monitoring to identify and report suspicious transactions and, on a risk basis, to maintain and update customer information. With respect to the new requirement to obtain beneficial ownership information, financial institutions will have to identify and verify the identity of any individual who owns 25 percent or more of a legal entity, and an individual who controls the legal entity. Based upon comments received in response to the proposed rule that was published in August 2014, the final rule extends the proposed implementation period from one year to two years, expands the list of exemptions, and makes use of a standardized beneficial ownership form optional as long as a financial institution collects the required information.

In addition to these customer due diligence final rules, the U.S. Treasury Department and the Internal Revenue Service (IRS) also released proposed regulations related to foreign-owned disregarded entities (i.e., single-member limited liability companies). These proposed regulations are intended to require information reporting by foreign-owned disregarded entities.

Appendix A

Entity Resolution

Entity resolution is the operational-process of determining whether two references to real-world objects are referring to the same, or to different, objects[23], e.g. a person, business, location or vessel. Entity resolution is also called record linkage, reference resolution and entity disambiguation.

There is a long history of work in entity resolution[24], with some of the earliest work going back to the 1950s. Entity resolution has received considerable attention in recent years[25], with the emergence of "big data" and the developments in the fields of artificial intelligence (especially machine learning and natural language processing).

In this appendix, the focus is on describing some challenges and opportunities in AML name/attribute matching against multiple data sources.

Entity resolution systems include rules engine(s) and workflow processes, which apply business intelligence, defined in elaborate algorithms, to the resolved identities and their relationships. These advanced technologies

---

23 John R. Talburt, "Entity Resolution and Information Quality", Morgan Kaufman, January 2011

24 Peter Christen, "Data Matching: Concepts and Techniques for Record Linkage, Entity Resolution, and Duplicate Detection", Springer, July 2012

25 John R. Talburt and Yinle Zhou, "Entity Information Life Cycle for Big Data: Master Data Management and Information Integration", Morgan Kaufmann, April 2015

can make automated decisions and impact business processes in real time, limiting the need for human intervention.

In this appendix, only the classical Soundex algorithm in entity resolution is briefly discussed. Further detailed discussions of more entity resolution mathematical and/or computer science algorithms could be found in references [74 - 78].

THE CLASSICAL SOUNDEX ALGORITHM

Soundex is a phonetic algorithm for indexing names by sound, as pronounced in English (and some other languages). The Soundex algorithm applies a series of rules to a word (or a string in the computer science terminology) to generate the four-character code. The encoding steps are as follows:

- Ignore all characters in the word being encoded except for the English letters, A to Z.

- Retain the first letter of the word and drop all other occurrences of A, E, I, O, U, H, W, Y.

- Assign a numeric digit between 1 and 6 to all letters after the first using the following mappings:

    ◦ 1: B, F, P or V

    ◦ 2: C, G, J, K, Q, S, X, Z

    ◦ 3: D, T

    ◦ 4: L

    ◦ 5: M, N

    ◦ 6: R

- Where adjacent digits are the same, remove all but one of those digits unless a vowel, H, W or Y was found between them in the original text.

- Force the code to be four characters in length by appending with zeros until there are three numbers (if the length of the result < 3) or by retaining the first 3 numbers (if the length of the result > 3).

By applying the classical Soundex algorithm, the Soundex code for both "Parade" and "Perrett" is P630:

- Soundex code of "Parade" = Soundex code of "Prd" = P63 appending with 0 = P630

- Soundex code of "Perrett" = Soundex code of "Prrtt" = P6633 removing duplicated adjacent digits = P63 appending with 0 = P630

There are many variations or enhanced versions of original Soundex algorithm, but like any other entity resolution algorithms, none of them are perfect: all versions of Soundex attempt to capture phonetic similarities without taking into account the surrounding context in which a word occurs, for example, they will fail to recognize equivalent but dissimilar name variants such as "Robert" versus "Bob".

It is worth mentioning that since Soundex codes have four characters, one could measure the similarity of two words by converting them to their Soundex codes and then reporting the number of matching code positions. The result (or the "score") ranges from 0 to 4, with 0 being no match and 4 being an exact match (thus "Parade" and "Perrett" is an "exact match" under the classical Soundex algorithm).

NAME/ATTRIBUTE MATCHING

As it was discussed in Chapter 3 and Chapter 5, financial institutions use watch-list screening and matching technology to accurately and efficiently check customers and transactions against sanctions, politically exposed persons (PEPs), and various external or internal reference lists or data sets. But there are many challenges and opportunities in name/attribute matching for AML compliance.

CHALLENGES

The challenges of entity resolution based name/attribute matching are to improve the effectiveness and efficiency by reducing or minimizing the false positives and false negatives to acceptable risk management thresholds.

A false positive is the case where a person or an entity that is incorrectly identified as a match. False positives of name/attribute matching against a "bad guy" watch-list are a significant burden to financial institutions since significant cost and effort are required to investigate each of these false positive alerts or hits.

A false negative is the case where a person or an entity is identified as a missed matches (e.g., as "safe" against a "bad guy" watch-list). False negatives of name/attribute matching, if beyond acceptable thresholds, could lead to enforcement actions and reputational risks for financial institutions.

NAME/ATTRIBUTE VARIATIONS

To reduce or minimize the false positives and false negatives, name/attribute matching engines not only need to know that "Beth", "Liz", and "Elizabeth" are all the same person, they also have to deal with cultural anomalies (first name/last name vs. last name/first name), honorifics, translations, and the like. The table below highlights some of the more common name/attribute variations encountered in real life.

Variation Type	Examples
Aliases (Weak Aliases/AKAs[26] include nicknames, noms de guerre, and unusually common acronyms. OFAC includes these AKAs because, based on information available to it, the sanctions targets refer to themselves, or are referred to, by these names.)	In the TXT and PDF versions of the OFAC SDN List: ALLANE, Hacene (a.k.a. ABDELHAY, al-Sheikh; a.k.a. AHCENE, Cheib; a.k.a. "ABU AL-FOUTOUH"; a.k.a. "BOULAHIA"; a.k.a. "HASSAN THE OLD"); DOB 17 Jan 1941; POB El Menea, Algeria (individual) [SDGT]
Cultural variations	Beth vs. Elizabeth; Bill vs. William.
Double first names	Jean-Claude vs. Jean Claude, or vs. Jean, or vs. Claude.
Double last names	Philips-Martin vs. Philips Martin, or vs. Philips, or vs. Martin.
Initials	M. J. Jackson vs. Michael J. Jackson, or vs. Michael Joseph Jackson
Interchanging of vowels	Hussein vs. Hussien
Name changes during the course of their life for individuals or entities	Nancy Davis Reagan vs. Anne Frances Robbins, after she married Ronald Reagan in 1952.
Nicknames	Mike vs. Mick, or vs. Mikey
Phonetic variations	Michel vs. Michal, or vs. Miguel
Re-ordered names (such as First name/Last name vs. Last name/ First name)	Ying Wang vs. Wang Ying
Spelling variations (including but not limited to typographical errors, substituted letters, omissions, additional letters, irregular plurals, concatenated names)	Smyth vs. Smith; Collins vs. Colins; Britney Spears vs. Brittany Spears; McDonald, vs. Mc Donald, or vs. MacDonald; Inukshuk vs. Inukshuit; Hua Guo Feng vs. Hua Guofeng

---

[26] U.S. Department of the Treasury, "Recent OFAC Actions - SDN Alias Screening Expectations" is available at
https://www.treasury.gov/resource-center/sanctions/OFAC-Enforcement/Pages/weak_strong_alias.aspx (retrieved on May 1, 2016)

Titles	Sheikh Abdul Rahman vs. Abdul Rahman
Transliterations/translations of foreign script names (such as names in Arabic, Chinese, Cyrillic and etc.)	Mohamed vs. Mohammed, or vs. Mohammad, or vs. Muhammed, or vs. Muhammad, or vs. Mahammad
Business entity name abbreviations	IBM vs. International Business Machines
Business entity name variations	Acme International vs. Acme Int'l
Professional designations	John Doe, Doctor of Dental Surgery vs. John Doe DDS
Address abbreviations	St. vs. Street; Lane vs. Ln.; Apartment vs. Apt.
Address synonyms	Manhattan, New York vs. New York City
Concatenated address	101 Bridge Point Avenue vs. 101 Bridgepoint Avenue
Switched unit numbers	808 - 1234 Elm Drive vs. 1234 Elm Drive, Apt. 808
Different date of birth (DoB) formats	mm/dd/yyyy vs. dd/mm/yyyy, or vs. dd/mm/yy
Missing DoB components	9/21/1970 vs. September 1970, or vs. 1970

Table-Appendix-A-1 Samples of Name/Attribute Variations

METRICS AND MEASURES

In entity resolution, some metrics are defined and used to measure the quality of record linkage (i.e., effectiveness measures).

Two more terms of entity resolution are defined below.

An entity that is correctly identified as a match is defined as a true positive.

An entity that is correctly not identified as a match (e.g., as "safe" against a "bad guy" watch-list) is defined as a true negative.

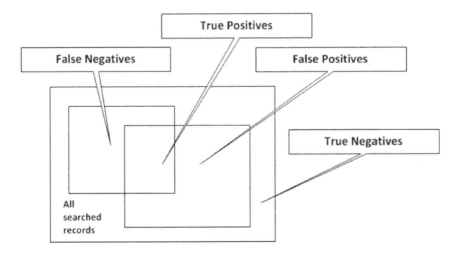

Figure-Appendix-A-1 Entity Resolution Measures

And if we define:

- TP = number of true positives.

- FP = number of false positives.

- TN = number of true negatives.

- FN = number of false negatives.

Then the entity resolution quality metrics are defined as follows:

- Precision = TP / (TP + FP)

- Recall = TP / (TP + FN)

- Harmonic mean (or F-measure)

= 2 * (Precision * Recall) / (Precision + Recall)

- Accuracy = [(TP + TN) / (TP + FP + TN + FN)]*100%

- Reduction ratio = 1 - Accuracy

- Match quality = TP / (TP + TN)

- Specificity = TN / (TN + FP)

Among those metrics, the most notable ones are Precision, Recall and Accuracy.

- Precision = the number of true positives that are correctly identified over the total number of all, correctly or not, identified positive results (i.e., the sum of the number of true positives and the number of false positives).

- Recall = the number of true positives that are correctly identified over the number of relevant records that are supposed to be matched.

- Accuracy = the proportion of all correctly identified results (both true positives and true negatives) among the total number of matching cases examined.

The efficiency of the name/attribute matching is commonly determined in terms of the execution time.

FALSE-POSITIVES/FALSE-NEGATIVES REDUCTION

In theory, if there are no false positives and no false negatives, then a name/attribute matching is up to the "gold standard" (i.e., with an accuracy of 100%). But in practice, neither entity resolution algorithms nor record data sets are perfect. It requires the improvement on both the information technology employed and governing compliance program to decrease the number of false positives and false negatives. In Chapter 5 some AML compliance improvement factors are discussed for reducing false positives and false negatives. Here are few technical factors that could be considered to reduce false positives and/or false negatives in name/attribute matching:

1. Choose or add proper data fields/match keys for the name/attribute matching. For example, leverage multiple entity attributes: in addition to the name, we could add gender, address (street address,

city, zip/postal code, state/province, and country), DoB, tax ID to the matching process.

Successful entity resolution of both individuals and businesses requires a solution that utilizes all of the available record data to improve the probability of a match.

2. Select a platform that supports federated matching algorithms.

    A name/attribute matching platform that only uses a very limited set of simple entity resolution algorithms may have many "blind spots" for name/attribute matching (we could see this by looking at common name/attribute variations mentioned above). A platform that is equipped with federated matching algorithms can function with multiple algorithms enabled and has the ability to turn on or off certain algorithms depending on business requirements.

3. Build and use white (or "exclusion") lists.

    Names/entities that have been identified as false positives against watch-lists should be "excluded" by adding to the match filter.

4. Continuous data quality improvement.

    The quality of the data (both the source data being compared and data records on the watch-lists) is a key to the accuracy and efficiency of matching process and needs to be optimized in an on-going basis.

We complete this appendix by giving two examples to show how to calculate the Precision, Recall and Accuracy for a watch-list matching/screening.

Assume the following:

*   A watch-list has 100,000 records

*   A data set contains 100 records that need to be checked against the watch-list

- Of 50 hits, 10 were "true matches" after the scanning results were examined

- 2 missed matches after examining the source data set

First, we could summarize the results as follows:

TP = 10; TN = (100 − 50) − 2 = 48; FP = 50 − 10 = 40; FN = 2

Then we could calculate the Precision, Recall and Accuracy as follows:

Precision = TP / (TP + FP) = 10 / (10 + 40) = 0.2

Recall = TP / (TP + FN) = 10 / (10 + 2) = 0.83

Accuracy = [(TP + TN) / (TP + FP + TN + FN)]*100%

= [(10 + 48) / (10 + 40 + 48 + 2)]*100%

= (58/100)*100%

= 58%

Assume the following after the data quality improvement and the addition of "exclusion" list:

- A watch-list has 100,000 records

- A data set contains 100 records that need to be checked against the watch-list

- Of 12 hits, 11 were "true matches" after the scanning results were examined (due to the addition of "exclusion" list and data quality improvement)

- 1 missed match after examining the source data set (due to the data quality improvement)

For the improved screening results, we could get:

TP = 11; TN = (100 – 12) – 1 = 87; FP = 12 – 11 = 1; FN = 1

Precision = TP / (TP + FP) = 11 / (11 + 1) = 0.92

Recall = TP / (TP + FN) = 11 / (11 + 1) = 0.92

Accuracy = [(TP + TN) / (TP + FP + TN + FN)]*100%

= [(11 + 87) / (11 + 1 + 87 + 1)]*100%

= (98/100)*100%

= 98%

Appendix B

Major Funds Transfer Systems

The main aspect of an AML transaction monitoring system is to monitor the money movement and information flow, therefore it is important to understand how funds get transferred within the financial infrastructure. In this appendix, an overview of formal funds transfer systems (opposite to informal value transfer systems (IVTS), such as Hawala[27]) in the U.S. and Canada is provided. The focus of this appendix is on wire transfers and Automated Clearing House (ACH) transfers.

Funds transfer systems are also called payments systems.

A funds transfer can generally be described as a series of payment instruction messages, beginning with the originator's (sending customer's) instructions, and including a series of further instructions between the participating institutions, with the purpose of making payment to the beneficiary (receiving customer).

Typically, payments go through two steps:

1. Clearing - the process of transmitting, reconciling and, in some cases, confirming payment orders prior to settlement. This process can include netting of payments and the establishment of final positions for settlement.

---

[27] An informal value transfer system (e.g., Hawalas) is a term used to describe a currency or value transfer system that operates informally to transfer money as a business.

2. Settlement - the release of payment obligations between two or more parties by transferring funds between them.

MAJOR FUNDS TRANSFER SYSTEMS IN THE UNITED STATES

Payment systems in the U.S. include mechanisms for processing both large-value wholesale and low-value retail funds transfers[28].

WHOLESALE PAYMENT SYSTEMS

At the wholesale level, two large-value electronic funds transfer systems, Fedwire Funds Service and Clearing House Interbank Payments System (CHIPS) settle the bulk of the dollar value of all payments in the U.S.

Fedwire Funds Service is a real-time gross settlement (RTGS) funds transfer system operated by the U. S. Federal Reserve Banks that enables financial institutions to electronically transfer funds. Real-time gross settlement means that the clearing and settlement of each transaction occurs continuously during the processing day.

An institution that maintains an account with a Federal Reserve Bank generally can become a Fedwire participant. Payment to the receiving participant (payee) over Fedwire Funds Service is final and irrevocable when the Federal Reserve Bank either credits the amount of the payment order to the receiving participant's Federal Reserve Bank reserve account or sends notice to the receiving participant, whichever is earlier. Payments via Fedwire Funds Service are continuously settled on an individual, order-by-order basis without netting.

The Fedwire funds transfer system serves as the primary domestic electronic funds transfer system in the United States. For example, on an average

---

[28]   Bank for International Settlements (BIS), "Payment, clearing and settlement systems in United States (Payment, clearing and settlement systems in the CPSS countries, Volume 2, pp 471 –508)", November 2012

day in September 2015, Fedwire Funds Service processed approximately 580,261 transactions valued at $3.4 trillion[29].

CHIPS is the largest private-sector U.S. dollar funds transfer system in the world, clearing and settling an average of $1.5 trillion in cross-border and domestic payments daily. It combines best of two types of payments systems: the liquidity efficiency of a netting system and the intraday finality of a RTGS system[30].

CHIPS is owned by financial institutions (49 Participants in 2015), and any banking organization with a regulated U.S. presence may become an owner and participate in the network.

The following steps outline how CHIPS works:

Step	Description (all in Eastern Time)
1	9 pm, CHIPS accounts at the Fed opens for pre-funding (Banks pre-fund required balances via Fedwire no later than 9 am) and CHIPS opens for processing payments.
2	9 pm to 5 pm, Banks send and receive payments
3	Prior to the daily cutoff time 5 pm, CHIPS nets and releases final payments (when an opportunity for settlement involving one, two or more payment orders is found).
4	Payments are final when released by CHIPS (throughout the day).
5	5 pm, CHIPS system removes credit limits and releases as many unresolved payments as possible (CHIPS nets any unresolved payments. Banks fund their respective negative closing position via Fedwire). 5:15 pm, CHIPS releases remaining payments.
6	5:15 pm, CHIPS sends payment orders to banks in positive closing positions via Fedwire.

Table-Appendix-B-1 CHIPS

---

[29] "Fedwire Funds Service - Monthly Statistics" is available at https://www.frbservices.org/operations/fedwire/fedwire funds services statistics.html (retrieved on May 1, 2016)

[30] https://www.theclearinghouse.org/payments/chips (retrieved on May 1, 2016)

Society for Worldwide Interbank Financial Telecommunication (SWIFT) is a global member-owned cooperative and the world's leading provider of secure financial messaging services. SWIFT messaging platform, products and services connect more than 11,000 banking and securities organizations, market infrastructures and corporate customers in more than 200 countries and territories. Whilst SWIFT does not hold funds or manage accounts or perform any form of clearing or settlement on behalf of customers, SWIFT does enable the global community of users to communicate securely, exchanging standardized financial messages in a reliable way, thereby facilitating global and local financial flows, and supporting trade and commerce all around the world. SWIFT directed funds transfers are actually settled through correspondent banking relationships, Fedwire, CHIPS, or other national payment systems.

The participating parties that may be involved in a funds transfer transaction include:

- Originator, e.g., individual, business entity - the initiator of a funds transfer;

- Beneficiary - the ultimate party to be credited or paid as a result of a funds transfer;

- Originator's Financial Institution - the financial institution receiving the transfer instructions from the originator and transmitting the instructions to the next party in the funds transfer;

- Beneficiary's Financial Institution - the financial institution that is to credit or pay the beneficiary party; and

- Additional Financial Institutions - other institutions that may be required to effect the transaction, such as intermediary banks (banks that act on behalf of the beneficiary bank), instructing banks (banks that initiate the fund transfer process).

A typical funds transfer involves an originator instructing its bank (the originator's bank) to make payment to the account of a payee (the beneficiary) with the beneficiary's bank.

The following diagram demonstrates how international wire works via Fedwire/SWIFT:

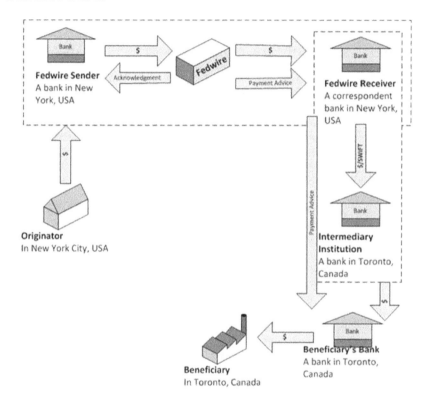

Figure-Appendix-B-1 Wire Transfers via Fedwire/SWIFT

The wire transfers via CHIPS/SWIFT work in a very similar way.

A cover payment occurs when the originator's bank and the beneficiary's bank do not have a relationship that allows them to settle the payment directly. In that case, the originator's bank instructs the beneficiary's bank to effect the payment and advises that transmission of funds to "cover" the obligation created by the payment order has been arranged through correspondent accounts at one or more intermediary banks. In the past,

SWIFT message protocols allowed cross-border cover payments to be effected by the use of separate, simultaneous message formats – the MT 103 and the MT 202. To address transparency concerns, SWIFT adopted a new message format for cover payments (the MT 202 COV) that contains mandatory fields for originator and beneficiary information. Effective November 21, 2009, the MT 202 COV is required for any bank-to-bank payment for which there is an associated MT 103.

The FFIEC BSA/AML Examination Manual provides the detailed information about Cover Payments, SWIFT message format MT 103, MT 202 and MT 202 COV for cross-border cover payments, Payable Upon Proper Identification (PUPID) transactions (PUPID transactions are funds transfers for which there is no specific account to deposit the funds into and the beneficiary of the funds is not a bank customer), Risk Factors/Mitigation for (wire) funds transfers.

RETAIL PAYMENT SYSTEMS

At the retail level, non-cash payments are processed through a number of systems, including cheque clearing systems, automated clearing house (ACH) systems and credit and debit card networks. But in this appendix, only the ACH payment network is discussed since it is a common form of electronic funds transfer used to make recurring and non-recurring payments.

An ACH is an electronic network for the exchange of payment instructions among financial institutions, typically on behalf of customers. ACH transactions are payment instructions to either debit or credit a deposit account. They are batch-processed, value-dated electronic funds transfers between originating and receiving financial institutions. ACH transactions can either be credits, originated by the account holder sending funds (payer), or debits originated by the account holder receiving funds (payee). ACH network moved almost $39 trillion and 22 billion electronic financial transactions in 2013.

The Federal Reserve (through the FedACH system) is one of the nation's two ACH operators; The Clearing House's Electronic Payments Network (EPN) is the sole private sector ACH operator. The National

Automated Clearing House Association (NACHA) is responsible for the administration, development, and enforcement of the NACHA Operating Rules and sound risk management practices for the ACH network.

An International ACH Transaction (IAT) is a debit or credit entry that is part of a payment transaction involving a financial agency located outside of the U.S.

In all ACH transactions, instructions flow from an originating depository financial institution (ODFI) to a receiving depository financial institution (RDFI). An ODFI may request or deliver funds. Transaction instructions and funds are linked using record keeping codes. If the ODFI sends funds, it is a credit transaction. If the ODFI requests funds, it is a debit transaction and funds flow in the opposite direction.

The following diagram shows how ACH works:

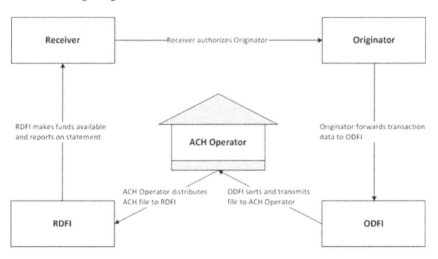

Figure-Appendix-B-2 ACH

Today, there is a slow, but certain global convergence toward ISO 20022, which is an ISO standard for electronic data interchange between financial institutions. As international regulators demand more detail from banks on payments to individuals and companies to ensure compliance with mandates. For example, the Financial Action Task Force (FATF) Special

Recommendation (SR) VII[31], which was originally issued in October 2001 and revised in February 2012, requires the inclusion of payer information throughout the payment chain. The more flexible ISO 20022 standard simplifies adherence to the standards of the AML laws and other regulatory rules. The industry needs a more flexible structure that allows information to pass end-to-end in a way that is easy to validate, and ISO 20022 offers the solution. Also global interoperability of real-time payments systems will require harmonization of market practices and standards.

In October 2013, a stakeholder group engaged an independent consultant to objectively evaluate the business case for or against adoption of ISO 20022 payments messages by U.S.-based payment clearing and settlement infrastructures, financial institutions and corporate customers. The stakeholder group includes the Federal Reserve, The Clearing House Payments Company L.L.C., NACHA – The Electronic Payments Association and the Accredited Standards Committee X9 – Financial Industry Standards, Inc. The stakeholder group will address the development of an implementation strategy for the application of the ISO 20022 standard to U.S. payment transactions as part of the desire to achieve greater end-to-end efficiency for domestic and cross-border payments.

In U.S., there are several specific AML compliance requirements for funds transfers, such as:

- OFAC sanction screening
- Funds Transfers Recordkeeping Requirements
- Travel Rule Requirements

For detailed AML compliance requirements for funds transfers, please consult the U.S. FFIEC Bank Secrecy Act (BSA)/ Anti-Money Laundering (AML) Examination Manual.

---

[31] FATF Recommendations are available at http://www.fatf-gafi.org/media/fatf/documents/recommendations/pdfs/FATF Recommendations.pdf (retrieved on May 1, 2016)

The FFIEC BSA/AML Examination Manual provides the detailed information about IAT, Third-Party Service Providers (TPSPs - entities other than an Originator, ODFI, or RDFI that perform any functions on behalf of the Originator, the ODFI, or the RDFI with respect to the processing of ACH entries), Risk Factors/Mitigation and OFAC Screening for ACH transactions.

MAJOR FUNDS TRANSFER SYSTEMS IN CANADA

There are two payments systems in Canada[32]:

- Large Value Transfer System (LVTS)

- Automated Clearing Settlement System (ACSS)

Both LVTS and ACSS systems are owned and operated by the Canadian Payments Association (CPA).

LVTS

The LVTS, operated by the CPA, is Canada's principal (wire transfers) system for large-value and time-sensitive payments. LVTS began full operations in February 1999. The system using the SWIFT network provides participants (17 participants in 2015) and their customers with the certainty that, once a payment message has passed the system's risk-control tests, it is final and irrevocable in real time. These transactions will settle on the books of the Bank of Canada at the end of the day. LVTS participants provide their customers, which include other financial institutions, as well as commercial and government entities, with indirect access to the system.

During 2009, LVTS processed, on average, 22,250 transactions per day worth approximately CAD 153 billion, which represents 90% of the total value in the Canadian national payments systems.

---

[32]   Bank for International Settlements (BIS), "Payment, clearing and settlement systems in Canada (Payment, clearing and settlement systems in the CPSS countries, Volume 1, pp 103 – 143)", September 2011

ACSS

The ACSS, introduced in 1984, is also owned and operated by the CPA. This uncollateralized deferred net settlement system clears and settles primarily retail electronic payments and paper-based payments in Canada. The ACSS is used to process a high volume of lower-value, less time-sensitive payments that do not require the intraday finality provided by the LVTS.

In 2013, the ACSS handled an average of 26.8 million payment items per day, with an average daily value of CAD $24 billion. Paper items accounted for 11 per cent of the volume and 49 per cent of the value, while electronic items made up about 89 per cent of the volume and 51 per cent of the value.

The CPA has embarked on a multi-year initiative to adopt an internationally recognized payment messaging standard ISO 20022 as part of a comprehensive strategy to modernize Canada's payment system.

In Canada, FINTRAC has the electronic funds transfers (EFTs) related guideline "Guideline 8: Submitting Electronic Funds Transfer Reports to FINTRAC", which explains when and how to submit electronic funds transfer reports. Actually there are three different versions of Guideline 8, by type of electronic funds transfer and reporting method.

- Guideline 8A: Submitting Non-SWIFT Electronic Funds Transfer Reports to FINTRAC Electronically

- Guideline 8B: Submitting SWIFT Electronic Funds Transfer Reports to FINTRAC

- Guideline 8C: Submitting Non-SWIFT Electronic Funds Transfer Reports to FINTRAC by Paper

For detailed Canadian Guideline 8 requirements, please consult the "Home > Guidance > Guidelines" section of FINTRAC web site:

http://www.fintrac-canafe.gc.ca/publications/guide/guide-eng.asp (retrieved on May 1, 2016)

Resources

References

1. Stefan D. Cassella, "Reverse Money Laundering", Journal of Money Laundering Control, Vol.7. No.1, pp.92 - 94, 2003

2. United Nations Office on Drugs and Crime (UNODC), "Estimating illicit financial flows resulting from drug trafficking and other transnational organized crimes", October 2011

3. Internal Revenue Service (IRS), "Examples of Money Laundering Investigations - Fiscal Year 2014", September 2015

4. Internal Revenue Service (IRS), "Examples of Money Laundering Investigations - Fiscal Year 2015", October 2015

5. Internal Revenue Service (IRS), "Examples of Money Laundering Investigations - Fiscal Year 2016", January 2016

6. Peter Reuter and Edwin M. Truman, "Chasing Dirty Money: Progress on Anti-Money Laundering", Peterson Institute, November 2004

7. Federal Financial Institutions Examination Council (FFIEC), "Bank Secrecy Act/ Anti-Money Laundering Examination Manual (2014 Edition) V2", February 2015

8. Financial Transactions and Reports Analysis Centre of Canada (FINTRAC), "FINTRAC Guidelines", all FINTRAC Guidelines

are available at http://www.fintrac.gc.ca/publications/guide/guide-eng.asp (retrieved on May 1, 2016)

9. Rachel Louise Ensign, "The Chemist Who Took On HSBC", The Wall Street Journal, February 29, 2016

10. Alan Katz and Dakin Campbell, "Inside the Money Laundering Scheme That Citi Overlooked for Years", Bloomberg Markets, November 20, 2015

11. Basel Committee on Banking Supervision (BCBS), "Sound management of risks related to money laundering and financing of terrorism", January 2014

12. KPMG, "Anti-Money Laundering Compliance Services for the banking industry", October 2007

13. John Atkinson, "Know Your Customer: Get it Right", American Bankers Association (ABA) Bank Compliance, Vol. 36 No. 6, pp 7 - 10, November-December 2015

14. Financial Transactions and Reports Analysis Centre of Canada (FINTRAC), "Guidance on the Risk-Based Approach to Combatting Money laundering and Terrorist Financing", May 2015

15. Financial Transactions and Reports Analysis Centre of Canada (FINTRAC), "FINTRAC Policy Interpretations : Ongoing Monitoring", May 2015

16. International Organization for Standardization (ISO), "ISO 19600:2014 Compliance management systems — Guidelines", December 2014

17. Office of the Superintendent of Financial Institutions (OSFI), "E-13 Guideline : Regulatory Compliance Management (RCM)", November 2014

18. Patrick Ryan, "The need for improvement", ACAMS Today, Vol. 11 No. 4, pp 38 – 40, September-November 2012

19. Carol Stabile, "A new approach to adverse media for enhanced due diligence", ACAMS Today, Vol. 13 No. 2, pp 72 – 74, March-May 2014

20. Financial Crimes Enforcement Network (FinCEN), "FinCEN's 314(a) Fact Sheet", February 2016

21. Financial Transactions and Reports Analysis Centre of Canada (FINTRAC), "Politically Exposed Foreign Person Determination", May 2015

22. LexisNexis, "Picture the power of deeper insight - Understand your BSA/AML risk profile with dynamic customer data", 2013

23. Oracle Corporation, "Hidden Relationships and Networks: Financial Institutions at Risk", October 2009

24. Jos de Wit, "A risk-based approach to AML: A controversy between financial institutions and regulators", Journal of Financial Regulation and Compliance, Vol. 15 No. 2, pp. 156 - 165, 2007

25. Allan G. Bluman, "Elementary Statistics: A Step by Step Approach (7th edition)", McGraw-Hill Higher Education, April, 2010

26. Financial Crimes Enforcement Network (FinCEN), "FinCEN Currency Transaction Report (FinCEN CTR) Electronic Filing Requirements Version 1.5", March 2015

27. Financial Crimes Enforcement Network (FinCEN), "FinCEN Suspicious Activity Report (FinCEN SAR) Electronic Filing Requirements Version 1.4", March 2015

28. Financial Crimes Enforcement Network (FinCEN), "BSA E-Filing System Batch File Testing Procedures Version 1.3", May 2012

29. Grant Thornton LLP, "Canada's compliance officers speak out - National Anti-Money Laundering survey report 2015", June 2015

30. KPMG International, "Global Anti-Money Laundering Survey 2014", February 2014

31. Dow Jones Risk & Compliance and Association of Certified Anti-Money Laundering Specialists (ACAMS), "2015 Global Anti-Money Laundering Survey', March 2015

32. LexisNexis and Association of Certified Anti-Money Laundering Specialists (ACAMS), "Current Industry Perspectives into Anti-Money Laundering Risk Management and Due Diligence", December 2015

33. Standish Group, "CHAOS Report 2015", 2015

34. Michael Bloch, Sven Blumberg, and Jürgen Laartz, "Delivering large-scale IT projects on time, on budget, and on value", McKinsey & Company, October 2012

35. Protiviti, "Views on AML Technology Vol. I, From System Selection to Effective Governance", November 2013

36. Protiviti, "Views on AML Technology Vol. II, Validation, Selection, Metrics and More", November 2014

37. Project Management Institute (PMI), "A Guide to the Project Management Body of Knowledge (PMBOK® Guide) Fifth Edition", May 2013

38. International Organization for Standardization (ISO), "ISO 21500:2012 Guidance on Project Management", September 2012

39. Project Management Institute (PMI), "Software Extension to the PMBOK® Guide Fifth Edition", January 2014

40. Kathy Schwalbe, "Information Technology Project Management 8th Edition", Course Technology, October 2015

41. Christine Bruce (West) and Yong Li, "RFP, WBS and COTS Implementation Planning", ISSIG Review, Vol. XIII No. 1, pp 12 – 14, Project Management Institute — Information Systems Specific Interest Group (ISSIG), 2009

42. PricewaterhouseCoopers LLP, "How to discover ways to sustainable anti-money laundering operations", 2008

43. Financial Transactions and Reports Analysis Centre of Canada (FINTRAC), "Policy Interpretations: Beneficial Ownership", May 2015

44. Financial Crimes Enforcement Network (FinCEN), Notice of Proposed Rulemaking (NPRM), "RIN 1506–AB25 Customer Due Diligence Requirements for Financial Institutions", August 2014

45. Ping He, "A typological study on money laundering", Journal of Money Laundering Control, Vol. 13 No 1, pp. 15 - 32, January 2010

46. Office of the Comptroller of the Currency (OCC) and Board of Governors of the Federal Reserve System (FRB), "Supervisory Guidance on Model Risk Management", April 2011

47. Rona Pocker and William Nayda, "Model Validation of Transaction Monitoring for Anti-Money-Laundering Activities", The Risk Management Association (RMA) Journal, Vol. 95 No. 6, pp 50 - 57, March 2013

48. Basel Committee on Banking Supervision (BCBS), "Principles for effective risk data aggregation and risk reporting", January 2013

49. Basel Committee on Banking Supervision (BCBS), "Enhancements to the Basel II framework", July 2009

50. Ernst & Young Global Limited, "BCBS 239 Risk data aggregation and reporting: A practical path to compliance and delivering business value", 2015

51. Deloitte LLP, "A guide to assessing your risk data aggregation strategies: How effectively are you complying with BCBS 239?", 2015

52. U.S. Department of the Treasury, "Frequently Asked Questions: Global Legal Entity Identifier (LEI)", August 2012

53. Superintendent of Financial Institutions (OSFI), "B-7: Derivatives Sound Practices", November 2014

54. Arin Ray and Neil Katkov, "Evaluating the Enterprise-Wide Compliance Vendors: Solutions for Anti-Money Laundering and Anti-Fraud", Celent, February 2012

55. Neil Katkov, "Evaluating the Vendors of Watchlist and Sanctions Solutions", Celent, April 2013

56. Arin Ray, "Emerging Solutions in Anti-Money Laundering Technology", Celent, May 2015

57. Julie Conroy, "AML: Smaller Financial Institutions in Search of Solutions", Aite Group, August 2014

58. Julie Conroy, "Global AML Vendor Evaluation: Managing Rapidly Escalating Risk", Aite Group, June 2015

59. Julie Conroy, "Watch-List Filtering Vendor Evaluation: Separating the Wheat From the Chaff", Aite Group, August 2015

60. Chartis Research, "Anti-Money Laundering Solutions 2013", April 2013

61. Chartis Research, "Financial Crime Risk Management Systems 2016", March 2016

62. Salvatore Cangialosi, "Outsourcing: Mercenary or Savior - What your Service Provider may not be telling you", ACAMS Today, Vol. 9 No. 3, pp 36 - 38, June–August 2010

63. Salvatore Cangialosi, Shaun M. Hassett, Arnie Scher and Eric A. Sohn, "Deal or No Deal? - Winning moves with vendors, consultants and other service providers" ACAMS Today, VoL. 10 No. 3, pp 22 - 24, June–August 2011

64. Salvatore Cangialosi, "The challenges of first generation rules", ACAMS Today, Vol. 11 No. 4, pp 12 - 13, September–November 2012

65. Mahesh Viswanathan, "Importance of data collection for a look-back", ACAMS Today, Vol. 8 No. 3, pp 46 - 47, June–August 2009

66. Óscar Marbán, Gonzalo Mariscal and Javier Segovia, "A Data Mining & Knowledge Discovery Process Model" (in "Data Mining and Knowledge Discovery in Real Life Applications", the book edited by: Julio Ponce and Adem Karahocá, pp 438 - 453), I-Tech, February 2009

67. EDRM LLC., "Electronic Discovery Reference Model (V3.0)", 2014

68. International Organization for Standardization (ISO)/ International Electrotechnical Commission (IEC), "ISO/IEC 12207:2008 Systems and software engineering -- Software life cycle processes", February 2008

69. International Organization for Standardization (ISO)/ International Electrotechnical Commission (IEC), "ISO/IEC 33001:2015 Information technology -- Process assessment -- Concepts and terminology", March 2015

70. International Software Testing Qualifications Board (ISTQB), "Certified Tester Foundation Level Syllabus", 2011

71. International Organization for Standardization (ISO)/ International Electrotechnical Commission (IEC), "27005:2011 Information technology -- Security techniques -- Information security risk management", Jane 2011

72. Simson L. Garfinkel, "NIST Internal or Interagency Reports (NISTIRs) 8053: De-Identification of Personal Information", National Institute of Standards and Technology (NIST), the U.S. Department of Commerce, October 2015

73. John Atkinson, "Four Keys to Maintaining an Effective AML Program", American Bankers Association (ABA) Bank Compliance, Vol. 35 No. 6, pp 8 - 14, November-December 2014

74. John R. Talburt, "Entity Resolution and Information Quality", Morgan Kaufman Publishing, January 2011

75. Peter Christen, "Data Matching: Concepts and Techniques for Record Linkage, Entity Resolution, and Duplicate Detection", Springer, July 2012

76. John R. Talburt and Yinle Zhou, "Entity Information Life Cycle for Big Data: Master Data Management and Information Integration", Morgan Kaufmann, April 2015

77. Chakkrit Snae, "A Comparison and Analysis of Name Matching Algorithms", International Journal of Computer, Electrical, Automation, Control and Information Engineering, Vol. 1, No. 1, pp 252 – 257, 2007

78. Frankie Patman and Leonard Shaefer, "Is Soundex Good Enough for You? The Hidden Risks of Soundex-Based Name Searching", IBM Global Name Recognition, 2006

79. Eric A. Sohn, "Original sins", ACAMS Today, Vol. 14 No. 2, pp 20 – 23, March–May 2015

80. Carol Stabile, "New directions in alert management : Winning the quality-quantity war", ACAMS Today, Vol. 12 No. 2, pp 40 – 41, March-May 2013

81. Bank for International Settlements (BIS), "Payment, clearing and settlement systems in United States (Payment, clearing and settlement systems in the CPSS countries, Volume 2, pp 471 – 508)", November 2012

82. Federal Financial Institutions Examination Council (FFIEC), "IT Examination Handbook - Wholesale Payment Systems", July 2004

83. Federal Financial Institutions Examination Council (FFIEC), "IT Examination Handbook - Retail Payment Systems", February 2010

84. Bank for International Settlements (BIS), "Payment, clearing and settlement systems in Canada (Payment, clearing and settlement systems in the CPSS countries, Volume 1, pp 103 – 143)", September 2011

85. International Organization for Standardization (ISO), "ISO 20022 Financial Services - Universal financial industry message scheme (Part 1 - Part 8)", May 2013

86. Financial Crimes Enforcement Network (FinCEN), "Feasibility of a Cross-Border Electronic Funds Transfer Reporting System under the Bank Secrecy Act", October 2006

87. U.S. Department of the Treasury, "National Money Laundering Risk Assessment 2015", June 2015

88. Department of Finance Canada, "Assessment of Inherent Risks of Money Laundering and Terrorist Financing in Canada", July 2015

89. Financial Crimes Enforcement Network (FinCEN), "Customer Due Diligence Requirements for Financial Institutions (Final Rules)", May 2016

Index

ASP – Application Service Provider, *90*

ATL – Above-the-Line, *110*

ATM/ABM – (U.S.) Automated Teller Machine/(Canadian) Automated Banking Machine, *83*

BAFO – Best and Final Offers, *61*

Balanced scorecard, *27*

Basel framework, *79*

BC – Business Continuity, *118*

BCBS – Basel Committee on Banking Supervision, *17*

BCBS 239, *78*

BCBS 275, *18*

BCP – Business Continuity Planning/Business Continuity Plan, *5, 118*

Beneficial ownership, *20, 72, 129*

BI – Business Intelligence, *103*

BIC – (SWIFT) Business Identifier Code, *84*

BIS – Bank for International Settlements, *144*

BOD – Board of Directors, *18*

BRD – Business Requirements Document, *86*

BSA – (U.S.) Bank Secrecy Act, *10*

BTL – Below-the-Line, *110*

CAD – Canadian dollar, *151*

CAMLO – Chief AML Officer, *54*

Canada Post, *84*

Canadian Criminal Code, *4*

Case-to-Alert ratio, *124*

CCO – Chief Compliance Officer, *25*

CD/GIC – (U.S.) Certificates of Deposit/(Canadian) Guaranteed Investment Certificate, *83*

CDD – Customer Due Diligence, *19*

CFPB – (U.S.) Consumer Financial Protection Bureau, *10*

CFPOA – (Canadian) Corruption of Foreign Public Officials Act, *4*

CFT/ATF – Combating the Financing of Terrorism/Anti-Terrorist Financing, *18/22*

CHIPS – (U.S.) Clearing House Interbank Payments System, *144*

CIA – (U.S.) Central Intelligence Agency/(Information security triad) Confidentiality, Integrity, Availability, *34/118*

CIF – Customer Information File, *104*

CIP – Customer Identification Program, *17*

Clearing, *143*

CMIR – (U.S.) Currency and Monetary Instruments Report/Report of International Transportation of Currency or Monetary Instruments, *12, 47*

MT – (SWIFT) Message Type, *50*

MT 103, *148*

MT 202, *148*

MT 202 COV, *50, 148*

NACHA – (U.S.) National Automated Clearing House Association, *149*

NAICS – North American Industry Classification System, *42*

NASCUS – (U.S.) National Association of State Credit Union Supervisors, *11*

NCUA – (U.S.) National Credit Union Administration, *10*

NDA – Non-Disclosure Agreement, *118*

NGO – Non-Governmental Organization, *21*

NIST – (U.S.) National Institute of Standards and Technology, *160*

NRA – (U.S.) Non-Resident Alien, *21*

OBS – Organizational Breakdown Structure, *65*

OCC – (U.S.) Office of the Comptroller of the Currency, *10*

ODFI – Originating Depository Financial Institution, *149*

OFAC – (U.S.) Office of Foreign Asset Control, *10*

OLA – Operational Level Agreement, *64*

OSFI – (Canadian) Office of the Superintendent of Financial Institutions, *13*

PCMLTFA – (Canadian) Proceeds of Crime (Money Laundering) and Terrorist Financing Act, *12*

www.ingramcontent.com/pod-product-compliance
Lightning Source LLC
Chambersburg PA
CBHW051239050326
40689CB00007B/992